James Russell Lowell

Fireside Travels

James Russell Lowell

Fireside Travels

ISBN/EAN: 9783337209926

Printed in Europe, USA, Canada, Australia, Japan

Cover: Foto ©Andreas Hilbeck / pixelio.de

More available books at **www.hansebooks.com**

BY

JAMES RUSSELL LOWELL.

"*Travelling makes a man sit still in his old age with satisfaction, and travel over the world again in his chair and bed by discourse and thoughts.*"
THE VOYAGE OF ITALY, by RICHARD LASSELS, Gent.

SIXTEENTH EDITION.

BOSTON AND NEW YORK:
HOUGHTON, MIFFLIN AND COMPANY.
The Riverside Press, Cambridge.
1889.

FIRESIDE TRAVELS.

THE greater part of this volume was printed ten years ago in "Putnam's Monthly" and "Graham's Magazine." The additions (most of them about Italy) have been made up, as the original matter was, from old letters and journals written on the spot. My wish was to describe not so much what I went to see, as what I saw that was most unlike what one sees at home. If the reader find entertainment, he will find all I hoped to give him.

To
W. W. S.

WHO carves his thought in marble will not scorn
These pictured bubbles, if so far they fly;
They will recall days ruddy but with morn,
Not red like these late past or drawing nigh!

CONTENTS.

	PAGE
CAMBRIDGE THIRTY YEARS AGO	3
A MOOSEHEAD JOURNAL	89
LEAVES FROM MY JOURNAL IN ITALY AND ELSEWHERE.	
AT SEA	155
IN THE MEDITERRANEAN	175
ITALY	187
A FEW BITS OF ROMAN MOSAIC	281

CAMBRIDGE THIRTY YEARS AGO.

A MEMOIR ADDRESSED TO THE EDELMANN STORG
IN ROME.

IN those quiet old winter evenings, around our Roman fireside, it was not seldom, my dear Storg, that we talked of the advantages of travel, and in speeches not so long that our cigars would forget their fire (the measure of just conversation) debated the comparative advantages of the Old and New Worlds. You will remember how serenely I bore the imputation of provincialism, while I asserted that those advantages were reciprocal; that an orbed and balanced life would revolve between the Old and the New as opposite, but not antagonistic poles, the true equator lying somewhere midway between them. I asserted also, that there were two epochs at which a man might travel, — before twenty, for pure enjoyment, and after thirty, for instruction. At twenty, the eye is sufficiently delighted with merely seeing; new things are pleasant only because they are not old; and we take everything heartily and naturally in the right way, — for even mishaps are like knives, that either serve us or cut us, as we grasp them by the blade or the handle. After thirty, we carry along our scales, with lawful weights stamped by experience, and our chemical tests acquired by study, with which to ponder and assay all arts, institutions, and manners, and to ascertain either their absolute worth or their merely relative value to ourselves. On the whole, I declared myself in favor of the after thirty method, — was it partly (so difficult is it to distinguish between opinions and personalities) because I had tried it myself, though with scales so imperfect and tests so inadequate? Perhaps so, but more because I held that a man should have travelled thoroughly round himself and the great *terra incognita* just outside and inside his own threshold, before he undertook voyages of discovery to other worlds. "Far countries he can safest visit who himself is doughty," says Beowulf. Let him first thoroughly explore that strange country laid down on the maps as SEAUTON; let him look down into its craters, and find whether they be burnt-out or only smouldering; let him know between the good and evil fruits of its passionate tropics; let him experience how healthful are its serene and high-lying table-lands; let him be many times driven back (till he wisely consent to be baffled) from its speculative northwest passages that lead mostly to the dreary solitudes of a sunless world, before he think himself morally equipped for travels to more distant regions. But does he commonly even so much as think of this, or, while buying amplest trunks for his corporeal apparel, does it once occur to him how very small a portmanteau will contain all his mental and spiritual outfit? It is more often true that a man who could scarce be induced to expose his unclothed body even to a village of prairie-dogs, will complacently display a mind as naked as the day it was born, without so much as a fig-leaf of acquirement on it, in every gallery of Europe, —

> "Not caring, so that sumpter-horse, the back,
> Be hung with gaudy trappings, in what coarse,
> Yea, rags most beggarly, they clothe the soul."

If not with a robe dyed in the Tyrian purple of imaginative culture, if not with the close-fitting, work-day dress of social or business training, — at least, my dear Storg, one might provide himself with the merest waist-clout of modesty!

But if it be too much to expect men to traverse and survey themselves before they go abroad, we might certainly ask that they should be familiar with their own villages. If not even that, then it is of little import whither they go; and let us hope that, by seeing how calmly their own narrow neighborhood bears their departure, they may be led to think that the circles of disturbance set in motion by the fall of their tiny drop into the ocean of eternity, will not have a radius of more than a week in any direction; and that the world can endure the subtraction of even a justice of the peace with provoking equanimity. In this way, at least, foreign travel may do them good, — may make them, if not wiser, at any rate less fussy. Is it a great way to go to school, and a great fee to pay for the lesson? We cannot give too much for the genial stoicism which, when life flouts us, and says, *Put that in your pipe and smoke it!* can puff away with as sincere a relish as if it were tobacco of Mount Lebanon in a *narghileh* of Damascus.

After all, my dear Storg, it is to know *things* that one has need to travel, and not *men*. Those force us to come to them, but these come to us, — sometimes whether we will or no. These exist for us in every variety in our own town. You may find your antipodes without a voyage to China; he lives there, just round the next corner, precise, for mal, the slave of precedent, making all his teacups with a break in the edge, because his model had one, and your fancy decorates him with an endlessness of airy pigtail. There, too, are John Bull, Jean Crapaud, Hans Sauerkraut, Pat Murphy, and the rest.

It has been well said:

> "He needs no ship to cross the tide,
>   Who, in the lives around him, sees
>   Fair window-prospects opening wide
>   O'er history's fields on every side,
>   Rome, Egypt, England, Ind, and Greece.
>
> "Whatever moulds of various brain
>   E'er shaped the world to weal or woe,
>   Whatever empires' wax and wane,
>   To him who hath not eyes in vain,
>   His village-microcosm can show."

But *things* are good for nothing out of their natural *habitat*. If the heroic Barnum had succeeded in transplanting Shakespeare's house to America, what interest would it have had for us, torn out of its appropriate setting in softly-hilled Warwickshire, which showed us that the most English of poets must be born in the most English of counties? I mean by a *Thing* that which is not a mere spectacle, that which some virtue of the mind leaps forth to, as it also sends forth its sympathetic flash to the mind, as soon as they come within each other's sphere of attraction, and, with instantaneous coalition, form a new product, — knowledge.

Such, in the understanding it gives us of early Roman history, is the little territory around Rome, the *gentis cunabula*, without a sight of which Livy and Niebuhr and the maps are vain. So, too, one must go to Pompeii and the *Museo Borbonico*, to get a true conception of that wondrous artistic nature of the Greeks, strong enough, even in that petty colony, to survive foreign conquest and to assimilate barbarian blood, showing a grace and fertility of invention whose Roman copies Rafaello himself could only copy, and enchanting even the base utensils of the kitchen with an inevitable sense of beauty to which we subterranean Northmen have not yet so much as dreamed of climbing. Mere sights one can see quite as well at home. Mont Blanc does not tower more grandly in the memory than did the dream-peak which loomed afar on the morning horizon of hope, nor did the smoke-palm of Vesuvius stand more erect and fair, with tapering stem and spreading top, in that Parthenopean air, than under the diviner sky of imagination. I know what Shakespeare says about homekeeping youths, and I can fancy what you will add about America being interesting only as a phenomenon, and uncomfortable to live in, because we have not yet done with getting ready to live. But is not your Europe, on the other hand, a place where men have done living for the present, and of value chiefly because of the men who had done living in it long ago? And if, in our rapidly-moving country, one feel sometimes as if he had his home on a railroad train, is there not also a satisfaction in knowing that one *is* going *some*where? To what end visit Europe, if people carry with them, as most do, their old parochial horizon, going hardly as Americans even, much less as men? Have we not both seen persons abroad who put us in mind of parlor gold-fish in their vase, isolated in that little globe of their own element, incapable of communication with the strange world around them, a show themselves, while it was always doubtful if they could see at all beyond the limits of their portable prison? The wise man travels to discover himself; it is to find himself out that he goes out of himself and his habitual associations, trying everything in turn till he find that one activity, that royal standard, sovran over him by divine right, toward which all the disbanded powers of his nature and the irregular tendencies of his life gather joyfully, as to the common rallying-point of their loyalty.

All these things we debated while the ilex logs upon the hearth burned down to tinkling coals, over which a gray, soft moss of ashes grew betimes, mocking the poor wood with a pale travesty of that green and gradual decay on forest-floors, its natural end. Already the clock at the *Cappuccini* told the morning quarters, and on the pauses of our talk no sound intervened but the muffled hoot of an owl in the near convent-garden, or the rattling tramp of a patrol of that French army which keeps him a prisoner in his own city who claims to lock and unlock the doors of heaven. But still the discourse would eddy round one obstinate rocky tenet of mine, for I maintained, you remember, that the wisest man was he who stayed at home; that to see the antiquities of the Old World was nothing, since the youth of the world was really no farther away from us than our own youth; and that, moreover, we had also in America things amazingly old, as our boys, for example. Add, that in the end this antiquity is a matter of comparison, which skips from place to place as nimbly as Emerson's Sphinx, and that one old thing is good only till we have seen an older. England is ancient till we go to Rome; Etruria dethrones Rome, but only to pass this sceptre of antiquity which so lords it over our fancies to the Pelasgi, from whom Egypt straightway wrenches it, to give it up in turn to older India. And whither then? As well rest upon the first step, since the effect of what is old upon the mind is single and positive, not cumulative. As soon as a thing is past, it is as infinitely far away from us as if it had happened millions of years ago. And if the learned Huet be correct, who reckoned that all human thoughts and records could be included in ten folios, what so frightfully old as we ourselves, who can, if we choose, hold in our memories every syllable of recorded time, from the first crunch of Eve's teeth in the apple downward, being thus ideally contemporary with hoariest Eld?

> "The pyramids built up with newer might
> To us are nothing novel, nothing strange."

Now, my dear Storg, you know my (what

the phrenologists call) inhabitiveness and adhesiveness, — how I stand by the old thought, the old thing, the old place, and the old friend, till I am very sure I have got a better, and even then migrate painfully. Remember the old Arabian story, and think how hard it is to pick up all the pomegranate-seeds of an opponent's argument, and how, as long as one remains, you are as far from the end as ever. Since I have you entirely at my mercy, (for you cannot answer me under five weeks,) you will not be surprised at the advent of this letter. I had always one impregnable position, which was, that, however good other places might be, there was only one in which we could be born, and which therefore possessed a quite peculiar and inalienable virtue. We had the fortune, which neither of us have had reason to call other than good, to journey together through the green, secluded valley of boyhood; together we climbed the mountain wall which shut in, and looked down upon, those Italian plains of early manhood; and, since then, we have met sometimes by a well, or broken bread together at an oasis in the arid desert of life, as it truly is. With this letter I propose to make you my fellow-traveller in one of those fireside voyages which, as we grow older, we make oftener and oftener through our own past. Without leaving your elbow-chair, you shall go back with me thirty years, which will bring you among things and persons as thoroughly preterite as Romulus or Numa. For so rapid are our changes in America that the transition from old to new, the shifting from habits and associations to others entirely different, is as rapid almost as the passing in of one scene and the drawing out of another on the stage. And it is this which makes America so interesting to the philosophic student of history and man. Here, as in a theatre, the great problems of anthropology — which in the Old World were ages in solving, but which are solved, leaving only a dry net result — are compressed, as it were, into the entertainment of a few hours. Here we have I know not how many epochs of history and phases of civilization contemporary with each other, nay, within five minutes of each other, by the electric telegraph. In two centuries we have seen rehearsed the dispersion of man from a small point over a whole continent; we witness with our own eyes the action of those forces which govern the great migration of the peoples now historical in Europe; we can watch the action and reaction of different races, forms of government, and higher or lower civilizations. Over there, you have only the dead precipitate, demanding tedious analysis; but here the elements are all in solution, and we have only to look to know them all. History, which every day makes less account of governors and more of man, must find here the compendious key to all that picture-writing of the Past. Therefore it is, my dear Storg, that we Yankees may still esteem our America a place worth living in. But calm your apprehensions; I do not propose to drag you with me on such an historical circumnavigation of the globe, but only to show you that (however needful it may be to go abroad for the study of æsthetics) a man who uses the eyes of his heart may find here also pretty bits of what may be called the social picturesque, and little landscapes over which that Indian-summer atmosphere of the Past broods as sweetly and tenderly as over a Roman ruin. Let us look at the Cambridge of thirty years since.

The seat of the oldest college in America, it had, of course, some of that cloistered quiet which characterizes all university towns. Even now delicately-thoughtful A. H. C. tells me that he finds in its intellectual atmosphere a repose which recalls that of grand old Oxford. But, underlying this, it had an idiosyncrasy of its own. Boston was not yet a city, and Cambridge was still a country village, with its own habits and traditions, not yet feeling too strongly the force of suburban gravitation. Approaching it from the west by what was then called the New Road (it is called so no longer, for we change our names whenever we can, to the great detriment of all historical association), you would pause on the brow of Symonds' Hill to enjoy a view singularly soothing and placid. In front of you lay the town, tufted with elms, lindens, and horse-chestnuts, which had seen Massachusetts a colony, and were fortunately unable to emigrate with the Tories by whom, or by whose fathers, they were planted. Over it rose the noisy belfry of the College, the square, brown tower of the church, and the slim, yellow spire of the parish meeting-house, by no means ungraceful, and then an invariable characteristic of New England religious architecture. On your right, the Charles slipped smoothly through green and purple salt-meadows, darkened, here and there, with the blossoming black-grass as with a stranded cloud-shadow. Over these marshes, level as water, but without its glare, and with softer and more soothing gradations of perspective, the eye was carried to a horizon of softly-rounded hills. To your left hand, upon the

Old Road, you saw some half-dozen dignified old houses of the colonial time, all comfortably fronting southward. If it were early June, the rows of horse-chestnuts along the fronts of these houses showed, through every crevice of their dark heap of foliage, and on the end of every drooping limb, a cone of pearly flowers, while the hill behind was white or rosy with the crowding blooms of various fruit-trees. There is no sound, unless a horseman clatters over the loose planks of the bridge, while his antipodal shadow glides silently over the mirrored bridge below, or unless,

> "O wingëd rapture, feathered soul of spring,
> Blithe voice of woods, fields, waters, all in one,
> Pipe blown through by the warm, mild breath of June
> Shepherding her white flocks of woolly clouds,
> The bobolink has come, and climbs the wind
> With rippling wings that quiver not for flight,
> But only joy, or, yielding to its will,
> Runs down, a brook of laughter, through the air."

Such was the charmingly rural picture which he who, thirty years ago, went eastward over Symonds' Hill had given him for

nothing, to hang in the Gallery of Memory
But we are a city now, and Common Councils have yet no notion of the truth (learned long ago by many a European hamlet) that picturesqueness adds to the actual money value of a town. To save a few dollars in gravel, they have cut a kind of dry ditch through the hill, where you suffocate with dust in summer, or flounder through waist-deep snow-drifts in winter, with no prospect but the crumbling earth-walls on either side. The landscape was carried away cart-load by cart-load, and, dumped down on the roads, forms a part of that unfathomable pudding, which has, I fear, driven many a teamster and pedestrian to the use of phrases not commonly found in English dictionaries.

We called it "the Village" then (I speak of Old Cambridge), and it was essentially an English village, quiet, unspeculative, without enterprise, sufficing to itself, and only showing such differences from the original type as the public school and the system of town govrnment might superinduce. A few houses, chiefly old, stood around the bare Common, with ample elbow-room, and old women, capped and spectacled, still peered through the same windows from which they had watched Lord Percy's artillery rumble by to Lexington, or caught a glimpse of the handsome Virginia General who had come to wield our homespun Saxon chivalry. People were still living who regretted the late unhappy separation from the mother island, who had seen no gentry since the Vassalls went, and who thought that Boston had ill kept the day of her patron saint, Botolph, on the 17th of June, 1775. The hooks were to be seen from which had swung the hammocks of Burgoyne's captive redcoats. If memory does not deceive me, women still washed clothes in the town spring, clear as that of Bandusia. One coach sufficed for all the travel to the metropolis. Commencement had not ceased to be the great holiday of the Puritan Commonwealth, and a fitting one it was, — the festival of Santa Scholastica, whose triumphal path one may conceive strewn with leaves of spelling-book instead of bay. The students (scholars they were called then) wore their sober uniform, not ostentatiously distinctive or capable of rousing democratic envy, and the old lines of caste were blurred rather than rubbed out, as servitor was softened into beneficiary. The Spanish king was sure that the gesticulating student was either mad or reading Don Quixote, and if, in those days, you met a youth swinging his arms and talking to himself, you might conclude that he was either a lunatic or one who was to appear in a "part" at the next Commencement. A favorite place for the rehearsal of these orations was the retired amphitheatre of the Gravel-pit, perched unregarded on whose dizzy edge, I have heard many a burst of *plusquam Ciceronian* eloquence, and (often repeated) the regular *saluto vos, præstantissimæ*, &c., which every year (with a glance at the gallery) causes a flutter among the fans innocent of Latin, and delights to applauses of conscious superiority the youth almost as innocent as they. It is curious, by the way, to note how plainly one can feel the pulse of self in the plaudits of an audience. At a political meeting, if the enthusiasm of the lieges hang fire, it may be exploded at once by an allusion to their intelligence or patriotism; and at a literary festival, the first Latin quotation draws the first applause, the clapping of hands being intended as a tribute to our own familiarity with that sonorous tongue, and not at all as an approval of the particular sentiment conveyed in it. For if the orator should say, "Well has Tacitus remarked, *Americani omnes quâdam vi naturæ furcâ dignissimi,*" it would be all the same. But the Gravel-pit was patient, if irresponsive; nor did the declaimer always fail to bring down the house, bits of loosened earth falling now and then from the precipitous walls, their cohesion perhaps overcome by the vibrations of the voice, and happily satirizing the effect of most popular discourses, which prevail rather with the earthy than the spiritual part of the hearer. Was it possible for us in those days to conceive of a greater potentate than the President of the University, in his square doctor's cap, that still filially recalled Oxford and Cambridge? If there was a doubt, it was suggested only by the Governor, and even by him on artillery-election days alone, superbly martial with epaulets and buckskin breeches, and bestriding the war-horse, promoted to that solemn duty for his tameness and steady habits.

Thirty years ago, the town had indeed a character. Railways and omnibuses had not rolled flat all little social prominences and peculiarities, making every man as much a citizen everywhere as at home. No Charlestown boy could come to our annual festival without fighting to avenge a certain tradicional porcine imputation against the inhabitants of that historic locality, and to which our youth gave vent in fanciful imitations of the dialect of the sty, or derisive shouts of "Charlestown hogs!" The penny newspaper had not yet silenced the tripod of the barber, oracle of news. Everybody knew everybody, and all about everybody, and village wit, whose high 'change was around the little market-house in the town square, had labelled every more marked individuality with nicknames that clung like burs. Things were established then, and men did not run through all the figures on the dial of society so swiftly as now, when hurry and competition seem to have quite unhung the modulating pendulum of steady thrift and competent training. Some slow-minded persons even followed their father's trade, — a humiliating spectacle, rarer every day. We had our established loafers, topers, proverb-mongers, barber, parson, nay, postmaster, whose tenure was for life. The great political engine did not then come down at regular quadrennial intervals, like a nail-cutting machine, to make all official lives of a standard length, and to generate lazy and intriguing expectancy. Life flowed in recognized channels, narrower perhaps, but with all the more individuality and force.

There was but one white-and-yellow-washer, whose own cottage, fresh-gleaming every June through grape-vine and creeper, was his only sign and advertisement. He was said to possess a secret, which died with him like that of Luca della Robbia, and certainly conceived all colors but white and yellow to savor of savagery, civilizing the stems of his trees annually with liquid lime, and meditating how to extend that candent baptism even to the leaves. His *pie-plants* (the best in town), compulsory monastics, blanched under barrels, each in his little hermitage, a vegetable Certosa. His fowls, his ducks, his geese, could not show so much as a gray feather among them, and he would have given a year's earnings for a white peacock. The flowers which decked his little *door-yard* were whitest China-asters and goldenest sunflowers, which last, backsliding from their traditional Parsee faith, used to puzzle us urchins not a little by staring brazenly every way except towards the sun. Celery, too, he raised, whose virtue is its paleness, and the silvery onion, and turnip, which, though outwardly conforming to the green heresies of summer, nourish a purer faith subterraneously, like early Christians in the catacombs. In an obscure corner grew the sanguine beet, tolerated only for its usefulness in allaying the asperities of Saturday's salt-fish. He loved winter better than summer, because Nature then played the whitewasher, and challenged with her snows the scarce inferior purity of his overalls and neck-cloth. I fancy that he never rightly liked Commencement, for bringing so many black coats together. He founded no school. Others might essay his art, and were allowed to try their prentice hands on fences and the like coarse subjects, but the ceiling of every housewife waited on the leisure of Newman (*ichneumon* the students called him for his diminutiveness), nor would consent to other brush than his. There was also but one brewer, — Lewis, who made the village beer, both spruce and ginger, a grave and amiable Ethiopian, making a discount always to the boys, and wisely, for they were his chiefest patrons. He wheeled his whole stock in a white-roofed handcart, on whose front a signboard presented at either end an insurrectionary bottle; yet insurgent after no mad Gallic fashion, but soberly and Saxonly discharging itself into the restraining formulary of a tumbler, symbolic of orderly prescription. The artist had struggled manfully with the difficulties of his subject, but had not succeeded so well that we did not often debate in which of the twin bottles Spruce was typified, and in which Ginger. We always believed that Lewis mentally distinguished between them, but by some peculiarity occult to exoteric eyes. This ambulatory chapel of the Bacchus that gives the colic, but not inebriates, only appeared at the Commencement holidays, and the lad who bought of Lewis laid out his money well, getting respect as well as beer, three *sirs* to every glass,—" Beer, sir? yes, sir: spruce or ginger, sir?" I can yet recall the innocent pride with which I walked away after that somewhat risky ceremony, (for a bottle sometimes blew up,) dilated not alone with carbonic acid gas, but with the more ethereal fixed air of that titular flattery. Nor was Lewis proud. When he tried his fortunes in the capital on Election-days, and stood amid a row of rival venders in the very flood of custom, he never forgot his small fellow-citizens, but welcomed them with an assuring smile, and served them with the first.

The barber's shop was a museum, scarce second to the larger one of Greenwood in the metropolis. The boy who was to be clipped there was always accompanied to the sacrifice by troops of friends, who thus inspected the curiosities *gratis*. While the watchful eye of R. wandered to keep in check these rather unscrupulous explorers, the unpausing shears would sometimes overstep the boundaries of strict tonsorial prescription, and make a notch through which the phrenological developments could be distinctly seen. As Michael Angelo's design was modified by the shape of his block, so R., rigid in artistic proprieties, would contrive to give an appearance of design to this aberration, by making it the key-note to his work, and reducing the whole head to an appearance of premature baldness. What a charming place it was,— now full of wonder and delight! The sunny little room, fronting southwest upon the Common, rang with canaries and Java sparrows, nor were the familiar notes of robin, thrush, and bobolink wanting. A large white cockatoo harangued vaguely, at intervals, in what we believed (on R.'s authority) to be the Hottentot language. He had an unveracious air, but what inventions of former grandeur he was indulging in, what sweet South-African Argos he was remembering, what tropical heats and giant trees by unconjectured rivers, known only to the wallowing hippopotamus, we could only guess at. The walls were covered with curious old Dutch prints, beaks of albatross and penguin, and whales' teeth fantastically engraved. There was Frederick the Great, with head drooped plottingly, and keen side-long glance from under the three-cornered hat. There hung Bonaparte, too, the long-haired, haggard general of Italy, his eyes sombre with prefigured destiny; and there was his island grave;— the dream and the fulfilment. Good store of sea-fights there was also; above all, Paul Jones in the Bonhomme Richard : the smoke rolling courteously to leeward, that we might see him dealing thunderous wreck to the two hostile vessels, each twice as large as his own, and the reality of the scene corroborated by streaks of red paint leaping from the mouth of every gun. Suspended over the fireplace, with the curling-tongs, were an Indian bow and arrows, and in the corners of the room stood New Zealand paddles and war-clubs, quaintly carved. The model of a ship in glass we variously estimated to be worth from a hundred to a thousand dollars, R. rather favoring the higher valuation, though never distinctly committing himself. Among these wonders, the only suspicious one was an Indian tomahawk, which had too much the peaceful look of a shingling-hatchet. Did any rarity enter the town, it gravitated naturally to these walls, to the very nail that waited to receive it, and where, the day after its accession, it seemed to have hung a lifetime. We always had a theory that R. was immensely rich, (how could he possess so much and be otherwise?) and that he pursued his calling from an amiable eccentricity. He was a conscientious artist, and never submitted it to the choice of his victim whether he would be perfumed or not. Faithfully was the bottle shaken and the odoriferous mixture rubbed in, a fact redolent to the whole school-room in the afternoon. Sometimes the persuasive tonsor would impress one of the attendant volunteers, and reduce his poll to shoe-brush crispness, at cost of the reluctant ninepence hoarded for Fresh Pond and the next half-holiday. So purely indigenous was our population then, that R. had a certain exotic charm, a kind of game flavor, by being a Dutchman.

Shall the two groceries want their *vates sacer*, where E. & W. I. goods and country prod*ooce* were sold with an energy mitigated by the quiet genius of the place, and where strings of urchins waited, each with cent in hand, for the unweighed dates (thus giving an ordinary business transaction all the excitement of a lottery), and buying, not only that cloying sweetness, but a dream also of Egypt, and palm-trees, and Arabs, in which vision a print of the Pyramids in our geography tyrannized like that taller thought of Cowper's?

At one of these the unwearied students

used to ply a joke handed down from class to class. *Enter A*, and asks gravely, "Have you any sour apples, Deacon?"

'Well, no, I haven't any just now that are exactly sour; but there's the bell-flower apple, and folks that like a sour apple generally like that." (*Exit A.*)

Enter B. "Have you any sweet apples, Deacon?"

"Well, no, I haven't any just now that are exactly sweet; but there's the bell-flower apple, and folks that like a sweet apple generally like that." (*Exit B.*)

There is not even a tradition of any one's ever having turned the wary Deacon's flank. and his Laodicean apples persisted to the end, neither one thing nor another. Or shall the two town-constables be forgotten, in whom the law stood worthily and amply embodied, fit either of them to fill the uniform of an English beadle? Grim and silent as Ninevite statues they stood on each side of the meeting-house door at Commencement, propped by long staves of blue and red, on which the Indian with bow and arrow, and the mailed arm with the sword, hinted at the invisible sovereignty of the state ready to reinforce them, as

> "For Achilles' portrait stood a spear
> Grasped in an armëd hand."

Stalwart and rubicund men they were, second only, if second, to S., champion of the county, and not incapable of genial unbendings when the fasces were laid aside. One of them still survives in octogenarian vigor, the Herodotus of village and college legend, and may it be long ere he depart, to carry with him the pattern of a courtesy, now, alas! old-fashioned, but which might profitably make part of the instruction of our youth among the other humanities! Long may R. M. be spared to us, so genial, so courtly, the last man among us who will ever know how to lift a hat with the nice graduation of social distinction! Something of a Jeremiah now, he bewails the decline of our manners. "My children," he says, "say, 'Yes sir,' and 'No sir'; my grandchildren, 'Yes' and 'No'; and I am every day expecting to hear 'D—n your eyes!' for an answer when I ask a service of my great-grandchildren. Why, sir, I can remember when more respect was paid to Governor Hancock's lackey at Commencement, than the Governor and all his suite get now." M. is one of those invaluable men who remember your grandfather, and value you accordingly.

In those days the population was almost wholly without foreign admixture. Two Scotch gardeners there were, — Rule, whose daughter (glimpsed perhaps at church, or possibly the mere Miss Harris of fancy) the students nicknamed Anarchy or Miss Rule, — and later Fraser, whom whiskey sublimed into a poet, full of bloody histories of the Forty-twa, and showing an imaginary French bullet, sometimes in one leg, sometimes in the other, and sometimes, toward nightfall, ir both. With this claim to military distinctior ne adroitly contrived to mingle another to a natural one, asserting double teeth all round his jaws, and, having thus created two sets of doubts, silenced both at once by a single demonstration, displaying the grinders to the confusion of the infidel.

The old court-house stood then upon the square. It has shrunk back out of sight now, and students box and fence where Parson once laid down the law, and Ames and Dexter showed their skill in the fence of argument. Times have changed, and manners, since Chief Justice Dana (father of Richard the First, and grandfather of Richard the Second) caused to be arrested for contempt of court a butcher who had come in without a coat to witness the administration of his country's laws, and who thus had his curiosity exemplarily gratified. Times have changed also since the cellar beneath it was tenanted by the twin-brothers Snow. Oyster men were they indeed, silent in their subterranean burrow, and taking the ebbs and flows of custom with bivalvian serenity. Careless of the months with an R in them, the maxim of Snow (for we knew them but as a unit) was, "When 'ysters are good, they *air* good; and when they ain't, they *is n't*." Grecian F. (may his shadow never be less!) tells this, his great laugh expected all the while from deep vaults of chest, and then coming in at the close, hearty, contagious, mounting with the measured tread of a jovial but stately butler who brings ancientest good-fellowship from exhaustless bins, and enough, without other sauce, to give a flavor of stalled ox to a dinner of herbs. Let me preserve here an anticipatory elegy upon the Snows written years ago by some nameless college rhymer.

DIFFUGERE NIVES.

Here lies, or lie, — decide the question, you,
If they were two in one or one in two, —
P. & S. Snow, whose memory shall not fade,
Castor and Pollux of the oyster-trade:
Hatched from one egg, at once the shell they burst,

(The last, perhaps, a P. S. to the first,)
So homoousian both in look and soul,
So undiscernibly a single whole,
That whether P. was S., or S. was P.,
Surpassed all skill in etymology;
One kept the shop at once, and all we know
Is that together they were *the* Great Snow,
A snow not deep, yet with a crust so thick
It never melted to the son of Tick;
Perpetual? nay, our region was too low,
Too warm, too southern, for perpetual Snow;
Still, like fair Leda's sons, to whom 't was given
To take their turns in Hades and in Heaven,
Our new Dioscuri would bravely share
The cellar's darkness and the upper air;
Twice every year would each the shades escape,
And, like a sea-bird, seek the wave-washed Cape,
Where (Rumor voiced) one spouse sufficed for both;
No bigamist, for she upon her oath,
Unskilled in letters, could not make a guess
At any difference twixt P. and S, —
A thing not marvellous, since Fame agrees
They were as little different as two peas,
And she, like Paris, when his Helen laid
Her hand 'mid snows from Ida's top conveyed
To cool their wine of Chios, could not know,
Between those rival candors, which was Snow
Whiche'er behind the counter chanced to be
Oped oysters oft, his clam-shells seldom he;

If e'er he laughed, 't was with no loud guffaw,
The fun warmed through him with a gradual thaw;
The nicer shades of wit were not his gift,
Nor was it hard to sound Snow's simple drift;
His were plain jokes, that many a time before
Had set his tarry messmates in a roar,
When floundering cod beslimed the deck's wet planks,—
The humorous specie of Newfoundland banks.

But Snow is gone, and, let us hope, sleeps well,
Buried (his last breath asked it) in a shell;
Fate with an oyster-knife sawed off his thread,
And planted him upon his latest bed.

Him on the Stygian shore my fancy sees
Noting choice shoals for oyster colonies,
Or, at a board stuck full of ghostly forks,
Opening for practice visionary Yorks.
And whither he has gone, may we too go, —
Since no hot place were fit for keeping Snow!

Jam satis nivis.

Cambridge has long had its port, but the greater part of its maritime trade was, thirty years ago, intrusted to a single Argo, the sloop Harvard, which belonged to the College, and made annual voyages to that vague

Orient known as Down East, bringing back the wood that, in those days, gave to winter life at Harvard a crackle and a cheerfulness, for the loss of which the greater warmth of anthracite hardly compensates. New England life, to be genuine, must have in it some sentiment of the sea, — it was this instinct that printed the device of the pine-tree on the old money and the old flag, — and these periodic ventures of the sloop Harvard made the old Viking fibre vibrate in the hearts of all the village boys. What a vista of mystery and adventure did her sailing open to us! With what pride did we hail her return! She was our scholiast upon Robinson Crusoe and the mutiny of the Bounty. Her captain still lords it over our memories, the greatest sailor that ever sailed the seas, and we should not look at Sir John Franklin himself with such admiring interest as that with which we enhaloed some larger boy who had made a voyage in her, and had come back without braces (*gallowses* we called them) to his trousers, and squirting ostentatiously the juice of that weed which still gave him little private returns of something very like sea-sickness. All our shingle vessels were shaped and rigged by her, who was our glass of naval fashion and our mould of aquatic form. We had a secret and wild delight in believing that she carried a gun, and imagined her sending grape and canister among the treacherous savages of Oldtown. Inspired by her were those first essays at navigation on the Winthrop duck-pond, of the plucky boy who was afterwards to serve two famous years before the mast. The greater part of what is now Cambridgeport was then (in the native dialect) a *huckleberry pastur.* Woods were not wanting on its outskirts, of pine, and oak, and maple, and the rarer tupelo with downward limbs. Its veins did not draw their blood from the quiet old heart of the village, but it had a distinct being of its own, and was rather a great caravansary than a suburb. The chief feature of the place was its inns, of which there were five, with vast barns and court-yards, which the railroad was to make as silent and deserted as the palaces of Nimroud. Great white-topped wagons, each drawn by double files of six or eight horses, with its dusty bucket swinging from the hinder axle, and its grim bull-dog trotting silent underneath, or in midsummer panting on the lofty perch beside the driver, (how elevated thither baffled conjecture,) brought all the wares and products of the country to their mart and seaport in Boston. These filled the inn-yards, or were ranged side by side under broad-roofed sheds, and far into the night the mirth of their lusty drivers clamored from the red-curtained bar-room, while the single lantern, swaying to and fro in the black cavern of the stables, made a Rembrandt of the group of ostlers and horses below. There were, beside the taverns, some huge square stores where groceries were sold, some houses, by whom or why inhabited was to us boys a problem, and, on the edge of the marsh, a currier's shop, where, at high tide, on a floating platform, men were always beating skins in a way to remind one of Don Quixote's fulling-mills. Nor did these make all the Port. As there is always a Coming Man who never comes, so there is a man who always comes (it may be only a quarter of an hour) too early. This man, so far as the Port is concerned, was Rufus Davenport. Looking at the marshy flats of Cambridge, and considering their nearness to Boston, he resolved that there should grow up a suburban Venice. Accordingly, the marshes were bought, canals were dug, ample for the commerce of both Indies, and four or five rows of brick houses were built to meet the first wants of the wading settlers who were expected to rush in — WHENCE? This singular question had never occurred to the enthusiastic projector. There are laws which govern human migrations quite beyond the control of the speculator, as many a man with desirable building-lots has discovered to nis cost. Why mortal men will pay more for a chess-board square in that swamp, than for an acre on the breezy upland close by, who shall say? And again, why, having shown such a passion for *your* swamp, they are so coy of *mine*, who shall say? Not certainly any one who, like Davenport, had got up too early for his generation. If we could only carry that slow, imperturbable old clock of Opportunity, that never strikes a second too soon or too late, in our fobs, and push the hands forward as we can those of our watches! With a foreseeing economy of space which now seems ludicrous, the roofs of this forlorn-hope of houses were made flat, that the swarming population might have where to dry their clothes. But A. U. C. 30 showed the same view as A. U. C. 1, — only that the brick blocks looked as if they had been struck by a *malaria*. The dull weed upholstered the decaying wharves, and the only freight that heaped them was the kelp and eel-grass left by higher floods. Instead of a Venice, behold a Torzelo! The unfortunate projector took to the last refuge of the unhappy — book-making, and bored the reluctant public with what he called a right-aim Testament, prefaced by a recommendation from General Jackson, who perhaps, from its title, took it for some treatise on ball-practice.

But even Cambridgeport, my dear Storg, did not want associations poetic and venerable. The stranger who took the "Hourly" at Old Cambridge, if he were a physiognomist and student of character, might perhaps have had his curiosity excited by a person who mounted the coach at the Port. So refined was his whole appearance, so fastidiously neat his apparel, — but with a neatness that seemed less the result of care and plan, than a something as proper to the man as whiteness to the lily, — that you would have at once classed him with those individuals, rarer than great captains and almost as rare as great poets, whom Nature sends into the world to fill the arduous office of Gentleman. Were you ever emperor of that Barataria which under your peaceful sceptre would present, of course, a model of government, this remarkable person should be Duke of Bienséance and Master of Ceremonies. There are some men whom destiny has endowed with the faculty of external neatness, whose clothes are repellent of dust and mud, whose unwithering white neck-cloths persevere to the day's end, unappeasably seeing the sun go down upon their starch, and whose linen makes you fancy them heirs in the maternal line to the instincts of all the washerwomen from Eve downward There are others whose inward natures possess this fatal cleanness, incapable of moral dirt spot. You are not long in discovering that the stranger combines in himself both these properties. A *nimbus* of hair, fine as an infant's, and early white, showing refinement of organization and the predominance of the spiritual over the physical, undulated and floated around a face that seemed like pale flame, and over which the flitting shades of expression chased each other, fugitive and gleaming as waves upon a field of rye. It was a countenance that, without any beauty of feature, was very beautiful. I have said that it looked like pale flame, and can find no other words for the impression it gave. Here was a man all soul, whose body seemed a lamp of finest clay, whose service was to feed with magic oils, rare and fragrant, that wavering fire which hovered over it. You, who are an adept in such matters, would have detected in the eyes that artist-look which seems to see pictures ever in the air, and which, if it fall on you, makes you feel as if all the world were a gallery, and yourself the rather indifferent Portrait of a Gentleman hung therein. As the stranger brushes by you in alighting, you detect a single incongruity, — a smell of dead tobacco-smoke. You ask his name, and the answer is, "Mr. Allston."

"Mr. Allston!" and you resolve to note

down at once in your diary every look, every gesture, every word of the great painter? Not in the least. You have the true Anglo-Norman indifference, and most likely never think of him again till you hear that one of his pictures has sold for a great price, and then contrive to let your grandchildren know twice a week that you met him once in a coach, and that he said, " Excuse me, sir," in a very Titianesque manner, when he stumbled over your toes in getting out. Hitherto Boswell is quite as unique as Shakespeare. The country-gentleman, journeying up to London, inquires of Mistress Davenant at the Oxford inn the name of his pleasant companion of the night before. " Master Shakespeare, an't please your worship." And the Justice, not without a sense of the unbending, says, " Truly, a merry and conceited gentleman!" It is lucky for the peace of great men that the world seldom finds out contemporaneously who its great men are, or, perhaps, that each man esteems himself the fortunate he who shall draw the lot of memory from the helmet of the future. Had the eyes of some Stratford burgess been achromatic telescopes, capable of a perspective of two hundred years! But, even then, would not his record have been fuller of *says I's* than *says he's*? Nevertheless, it is curious to consider from what infinitely varied points of view we might form our estimate of a great man's character, when we remember that he had his points of contact with the butcher, the baker, and the candlestick-maker, as well as with the ingenious A, the sublime B, and the Right Honorable C. If it be true that no man ever clean forgets everything, and that the act of drowning (as is asserted) forthwith brightens up all those o'er-rusted impressions, would it not be a curious experiment, if, after a remarkable person's death, the public, eager for minutest particulars, should gather together all who had ever been brought into relations with him, and, submerging them to the hair's-breadth hitherward of the drown ing-point, subject them to strict cross-examination by the Humane Society, as soon as they become conscious between the resuscitating blankets? All of us probably have brushed against destiny in the street, have shaken hands with it, fallen asleep with it in railway carriages, and knocked heads with it in some one or other of its yet unrecognized incarnations.

Will it seem like presenting a tract to a *colporteur*, my dear Storg, if I say a word or two about an artist to you over there in Italy? Be patient, and leave your button in my grasp yet a little longer. A person whose opinion is worth having once said to me, that, however one's notions might be modified by going to Europe, one always came back with a higher esteem for Allston. Certainly he is thus far the greatest English painter of historical subjects. And only consider how strong must have been the artistic bias in him, to have made him a painter at all under the circumstances. There were no traditions of art, so necessary for guidance and inspiration. Blackburn, Smibert, Copley, Trumbull, Stuart, — it was, after all, but a Brentford sceptre which their heirs could aspire to, and theirs were not names to conjure with, like those from which Fame, as through a silver trumpet, had blown for three centuries. Copley and Stuart were both remarkable men; but the one painted like an inspired silk-mercer, and the other seems to have mixed his colors with the claret of which he and his generation were so fond. And what could a successful artist hope for, at that time, beyond the mere wages of his work? His picture would hang in cramped back-parlors, between deadly cross-fires of lights, sure of the garret or the auction-room erelong, in a country where the nomad population carry no household gods with them but their five wits and their ten fingers. As a race, we care nothing about Art; but the Puritan and the Quaker are the only Englishmen who have had pluck enough to confess it. If it were surprising that Allston should have become a painter at all, how almost miraculous that he should have been a great and original one! We call him original deliberately, because, though his school is essentially Italian, it is of less consequence where a man buys his tools, than what use he makes of them. Enough English artists went to Italy and came back painting history in a very Anglo-Saxon manner, and creating a school as melodramatic as the French, without its perfection in technicalities. But Allston carried thither a nature open on the southern side, and brought it back so steeped in rich Italian sunshine that the east winds (whether physical or intellectual) of Boston and the dusts of Cambridgeport assailed it in vain. To that bare wooden studio one might go to breathe Venetian air, and, better yet, the very spirit wherein the elder brothers of Art labored, etherealized by metaphysical speculation, and sublimed by religious fervor. The beautiful old man! Here was genius with no volcanic explosions (the mechanic result of vulgar gunpowder often), but lovely as a Lapland night; here was fame, not sought after nor worn in any cheap French fashion as a ribbon at the button-hole, but so gentle, so retiring, that it seemed no more than an assured and emboldened modesty; here was ambition, undebased by rivalry and incapable of the sidelong look; and all these massed and harmonized together into a purity and depth of character, into a *tone*, which made the daily life of the man the greatest masterpiece of the artist.

But let us go back to the Old Town. Thirty years since, the Muster and the Cornwallis allowed some vent to those natural instincts which Puritanism scotched, but not killed. The Cornwallis had entered upon the estates of the old Guy-Fawkes procession, confiscated by the Revolution. It was a masquerade, in which that grave and suppressed humor, of which the Yankees are fuller than other people, burst through all restraints, and disported itself in all the wildest vagaries of fun. Commonly the Yankee in his pleasures suspects the presence of Public Opinion as a detective, and accordingly is apt to pinion himself in his Sunday suit. It is a curious commentary on the artificiality of our lives, that men must be disguised and masked before they will venture into the obscurer corners of their individuality, and display the true features of their nature. One remarked it in the Carnival, and one especially noted it here among a race naturally self-restrained; for Silas and Ezra and Jonas were not only disguised as Redcoats, Continentals, and Indians, but not unfrequently disguised in drink also. It is a question whether the Lyceum, where the public is obliged to comprehend all vagrom men, supplies the place of the old popular amusements. A hundred and fifty years ago, Cotton Mather bewails the carnal attractions of the tavern and the training-field, and tells of an old Indian who imperfectly understood the Eng lish tongue, but desperately mastered enough of it (when under sentence of death) to express a desire for instant hemp rather than listen to any more ghostly consolations. Puritanism — I am perfectly aware how great a debt we owe it — tried over again the old experiment of driving out nature with a pitchfork, and had the usual success. It was like a ship inwardly on fire, whose hatches must be kept hermetically battened down; for the admittance of an ounce of Heaven's own natural air would explode it utterly. Morals can never be safely embodied in the constable. Polished, cultivated, fascinating Mephistopheles! it is for the ungovernable breakings-away of the soul from unnatural compressions that thou waitest with a deprecatory smile. Then it is that thou offerest thy gentlemanly arm to unguarded youth for a pleasant stroll through the City of Destruction, and, as a special favor, introducest him to the bewitching Miss Circe, and to that model of the hospitable old English gentleman, Mr. Comus

But the Muster and the Cornwallis were not peculiar to Cambridge. Commencement-day was. Saint Pedagogus was a worthy whose feast could be celebrated by men who quarrelled with minced-pies, and blasphemed custard through the nose. The holiday preserved all the features of an English fair. Stations were marked out beforehand by the town constables, and distinguished by numbered stakes. These were assigned to the different venders of small wares and exhibiters of rarities, whose canvas booths, beginning at the market-place, sometimes half encircled the Common with their jovial embrace. Now all the Jehoiada-boxes in town were forced to give up their rattling deposits of specie, if not through the legitimate orifice, then to the brute force of the hammer. For hither were come all the wonders of the world, making the Arabian Nights seem possible, and which we beheld for half price; not without mingled emotions, — pleasure at the economy, and shame at not paying the more manly fee.

Here the mummy unveiled her withered charms, — a more marvellous Ninon, still attractive in her three-thousandth year. Here were the Siamese twins; ah! if all such forced and unnatural unions were made a show of! Here were the flying horses (their supernatural effect injured — like that of some poems — by the visibility of the man who turned the crank), on which, as we tilted at the ring, we felt our shoulders tingle with the *accolade*, and heard the clink of golden spurs at our heels. Are the realities of life ever worth half so much as its cheats? And are there any feasts half so filling at the price as those Barmecide ones spread for us by Imagination? Hither came the Canadian giant, surreptitiously seen, without price, as he alighted, in broad day, (giants were always foolish,) at the tavern. Hither came the great horse Columbus, with shoes two inches thick, and more wisely introduced by night. In the trough of the town-pump might be seen the mermaid, its poor monkey's head carefully sustained above water, to keep it from drowning. There were dwarfs, also, who danced and sang, and many a proprietor regretted the transaudient properties of canvas, which allowed the frugal public to share in the melody without entering the booth. Is it a slander of J. H., who reports that he once saw a deacon, eminent for psalmody, lingering near one of those vocal tents, and, with an assumed air of abstraction, furtively drinking in, with unhabitual ears, a song, not secular merely, but with a dash of libertinism? The New England proverb says, "All deacons are good, but — there's odds in deacons." On these days Snow became superterranean, and had a stand in the square, and Lewis temperately contended with the stronger fascinations of egg-pop. But space would fail me to make a catalogue of everything. No doubt, Wisdom also, as usual, had her quiet booth at the corner of some street, without entrance-fee, and, even at that rate, got never a customer the whole day long. For the bankrupt afternoon there were peep-shows, at a cent each.

But all these shows and their showmen are as clean gone now as those of Cæsar and Timour and Napoleon, for which the world paid dearer. They are utterly gone out, not leaving so much as a snuff behind, — as little thought of now as that John Robins, who was once so considerable a phenomenon as to be esteemed the last great Antichrist and son of perdition by the entire sect of Muggletonians. Were Commencement what it used to be, I should be tempted to take a booth myself, and try an experiment recommended by a satirist of some merit, whose works were long ago dead and (I fear) deedeed to boot.

"Menenius, thou who fain wouldst know how calmly men
 can pass
Those biting portraits of themselves, disguised as fox or
 ass, —
Go borrow coin enough to buy a full-length psyche-glass,
Engage a rather darkish room in some well-sought position,
And let the town break out with bills, so much per head
 admission, —
GREAT NATURAL CURIOSITY!! THE BIGGEST LIVING
 FOOL!!
Arrange your mirror cleverly, before it set a stool,

Admit the public one by one, place each upon the seat,
Draw up the curtain, let him look his fill, and then retreat.
Smith mounts and takes a thorough view, then comes serenely down,
Goes home and tells his wife the thing is curiously like Brown;
Brown goes and stares, and tells his wife the wonder's core and pith
Is that 't is just the counterpart of that conceited Smith.
Life calls us all to such a show : Menenius, trust in me,
While thou to see thy neighbor smil'st, he does the same for thee."

My dear Storg, would you come to my show, and, instead of looking in my glass, insist on taking your money's worth in staring at the exhibitor?

Not least among the curiosities which the day brought together were some of the graduates, posthumous men, as it were, disentombed from country parishes and district-schools, but perennial also, in whom freshly survived all the college jokes, and who had no intelligence later than their Senior year. These had gathered to eat the College dinner, and to get the Triennial Catalogue (their *libro d'oro*), referred to oftener than any volume but the Concordance. Aspiring men they were certainly, but in a right unworldly way; this scholastic festival opening a peaceful path to the ambition which might else have devastated mankind with Prolusions on the Pentateuch, or Genealogies of the Dormouse Family. For since in the academic processions the classes are ranked in the order of their graduation, and he has the best chance at the dinner who has the fewest teeth to eat it with, so, by degrees, there springs up a competition in longevity, — the prize contended for being the oldest surviving graduateship. This is an office, it is true, without emolument, but having certain advantages, nevertheless. The incumbent, if he come to Commencement, is a prodigious lion, and commonly gets a paragraph in the newspapers once a year with the (fiftieth) last survivor of Washington's Life-Guard. If a clergyman, he is expected to ask a blessing and return thanks at the dinner, a function which he performs with centenarian longanimity, as if he reckoned the ordinary life of man to be fivescore years, and that a grace must be long to reach so far away as heaven. Accordingly, this silent race is watched, on the course of the Catalogue, with an interest worthy of Newmarket; and as star after star rises in the galaxy of death, till one name is left alone, an oasis of life in the stellar desert, it grows solemn. The natural feeling is reversed, and it is the solitary life that becomes sad and monitory, the Stylites there on the lonely top of his century-pillar, who has heard the passing-bell of youth, love, friendship, hope, — of everything but immitigable eld.

Dr. K. was President of the University then, a man of genius, but of genius that evaded utilization, — a great water-power, but without rapids, and flowing with too smooth and gentle a current to be set turning wheels and whirling spindles. His was not that restless genius of which the man seems to be merely the representative, and which wreaks itself in literature or politics, but of that milder sort, quite as genuine, and perhaps of more contemporaneous value, which *is* the man, permeating the whole life with placid force, and giving to word, look, and gesture a meaning only justifiable by our belief in a reserved power of latent reinforcement. The man of talents possesses them like so many tools, does his job with them, and there an end; but the man of genius is possessed by it, and it makes him into a book or a life according to its whim. Talent takes the existing moulds, and makes its castings, better or worse, of richer or baser metal, according to knack and opportunity; but genius is always shaping new ones, and runs the man in them, so that there is always that human feel in its results which gives us a kindred thrill. *What* it will make, we can only conjecture, contented always with knowing the infinite balance of possibility against which it can draw at pleasure. Have you ever seen a man whose cheek would be honored for a million pay his toll of one cent? and has not that bit of copper, no bigger than your own, and piled with it by the careless toll-man, given you a tingling vision of what golden bridges *he* could pass, — into what Elysian regions of taste and enjoyment and culture, barred to the rest of us? Something like it is the impression made by such characters as K.'s on those who come in contact with them.

There was that in the soft and rounded (I had almost said melting) outlines of his face which reminded one of Chaucer. The head had a placid yet dignified droop like his. He was an anachronism, fitter to have been Abbot of Fountains or Bishop Golias, courtier and priest, humorist and lord spiritual, all in one, than for the mastership of a provincial college, which combined, with its purely scholastic functions, those of accountant and chief of police. For keeping books he was incompetent (unless it were those he borrowed), and the only discipline he exercised was by the unobtrusive pressure of a gentlemanliness which rendered insubordination to *him* impossible. But the world always judges a man (and rightly enough, too) by his little faults, which he shows a hundred times a day, rather than by his great virtues, which he discloses perhaps but once in a lifetime, and to a single person, — nay, in proportion as they are rarer, and he is nobler, is shyer of letting their existence be known at all. He was one of those misplaced persons whose misfortune it is that their lives overlap two distinct eras, and are already so impregnated with one that they can never be in healthy sympathy with the other. Born when the New England clergy were still an establishment and an aristocracy, and when office was almost always for life, and often hereditary, he lived to be thrown upon a time when avocations of all colors might be shuffled together in the life of one man, like a pack of cards, so that you could not prophesy that he who was ordained to-day might not accept a colonelcy of filibusters to-morrow. Such temperaments as his attach themselves, like barnacles, to what seems permanent; but presently the good ship Progress weighs anchor, and whirls them away from drowsy tropic inlets to arctic waters of unnatural ice. To such crustaceous natures, created to cling upon the immemorial rock amid softest mosses, comes the bustling Nineteenth Century and says, "Come, come, bestir yourself and be practical! get out of that old shell of yours forthwith!" Alas! to get out of the shell is to die!

One of the old travellers in South America tells of fishes that built their nests in trees (*piscium et summa hæsit genus ulmo*), and gives a print of the mother fish upon her nest, while her mate mounts perpendicularly to her without aid of legs or wings. Life shows plenty of such incongruities between a man's place and his nature, (not so easily got over as by the traveller's undoubting engraver,) and one cannot help fancying that K. was an instance in point. He never encountered, one would say, the attraction proper to draw out his native force. Certainly, few men who impressed others so strongly, and of whom so many good things are remembered, left less behind them to justify contemporary estimates. He printed nothing, and was, perhaps, one of those the electric sparkles of whose brains, discharged naturally and healthily in conversation, refuse to pass through the nonconducting medium of the inkstand. His *ana* would make a delightful collection. One or two of his official ones will be in place here. Hearing that Porter's flip (which was exemplary) had too great an attraction for the collegians, he resolved to investigate the matter himself. Accordingly, entering the old inn one day, he called for a mug of it, and, having drunk it, said, "And so, Mr. Porter, the young gentlemen come to drink your flip, do they?" "Yes, sir, — sometimes." "Ah, well, I should think they would. Good day, Mr. Porter," and departed, saying nothing more; for he always wisely allowed for tne existence of a certain amount of human nature in ingenuous youth. At another time the " Harvard Washington " asked leave to go into Boston to a collation which had been offered them. " Certainly, young gentlemen," said the President, " but have you engaged any one to bring home your muskets?" — the College being responsible for these weapons, which belonged to the State. Again, when a student came with a physician's certificate, and asked leave of absence, K. granted it at once, and then added, " By the way, Mr. ——, persons interested in the relation which exists between states of the atmosphere and health have noticed a curious fact in regard to the climate of Cambridge, especially within the College limits, — the very small number of deaths in proportion to the cases of dangerous illness." This is told of Judge W., himself a wit, and capable of enjoying the humorous delicacy of the reproof.

Shall I take Brahmin Alcott's favorite

word, and call him a dæmonic man? No, the Latin *genius* is quite old-fashioned enough for me, means the same thing, and its deriva tive *geniality* expresses, moreover, the base of K.'s being. How he suggested cloistered repose, and quadrangles mossy with centurial associations! How easy he was, and how without creak was every movement of his mind! This life was good enough for him, and the next not too good. The gentleman-like pervaded even his prayers. His were not the manners of a man of the world, nor of a man of the other world either; but both met in him to balance each other in a beautiful equilibrium. Praying, he leaned forward upon the pulpit-cushion as for conversation, and seemed to feel himself (without irreverence) on terms of friendly, but courteous, familiarity with Heaven. The expression of his face was that of tranquil contentment, and he appeared less to be supplicating expected mercies than thankful for those already found, — as if he were saying the *gratias* in the refectory of the Abbey of Theleme. Under him flourished the Harvard Washington Corps, whose gyrating banner, inscribed *Tam Marti quam Mercurio* (*atqui magis Lyœo* should have been added), on the evening of training-days, was an accurate dynamometer of Willard's punch or Porter's flip. It was they who, after being royally entertained by a maiden lady of the town, entered in their orderly book a vote that Miss Blank was a gentleman. I see them now, returning from the imminent deadly breach of the law of Rechab, unable to form other than the serpentine line of beauty, while their officers, brotherly rather than imperious, instead of reprimanding, tearfully embraced the more eccentric wanderers from military precision. Under him the Med. Facs. took their equal place among the learned societies of Europe, numbering among their grateful honorary members Alexander, Emperor of all the Russias, who (if College legends may be trusted) sent them in return for their diploma a gift of medals confiscated by the authorities. Under him the College fire-engine was vigilant and active in suppressing any tendency to spontaneous combustion among the Freshmen, or rushed wildly to imaginary conflagrations, generally in a direction where punch was to be had. All these useful conductors for the natural electricity of youth, dispersing it or turning it harmlessly into the earth, are taken away now, — wisely or not, is questionable.

An academic town, in whose atmosphere there is always something antiseptic, seems naturally to draw to itself certain varieties and to preserve certain humors (in the Ben Jonsonian sense) of character, — men who come not to study so much as to be studied. At the head-quarters of Washington once, and now of the Muses, lived C——, but before the date of these recollections. Here for seven years (as the law was then) he made his house his castle, sunning himself in his elbow-chair at the front-door, on that seventh day, secure from every arrest but Death's.

Here long survived him his turbaned widow, studious only of Spinoza, and refusing to molest the canker-worms that annually disleaved her elms, because we were all vermicular alike. She had been a famous beauty once, but the canker years had left her leafless, too; and I used to wonder, as I saw her sitting always alone at her accustomed window, whether she were ever visited by the reproachful shade of him who (in spite of Rosalind) died broken-hearted for her in her radiant youth.

And this reminds me of J. F., who, also crossed in love, allowed no mortal eye to behold his face for many years. The eremitic instinct is not peculiar to the Thebais, as many a New England village can testify; and it is worthy of consideration that the Romish Church has not forgotten this among her other points of intimate contact with human nature. F. became purely vespertinal, never stirring abroad till after dark. He occupied two rooms, migrating from one to the other, as the necessities of housewifery demanded, thus shunning all sight of womankind, and being practically more solitary in his dual apartment than Montaigne's Dean of St. Hilaire in his single one. When it was requisite that he should put his signature to any legal instrument, (for he was an anchorite of ample means,) he wrapped himself in a blanket, allowing nothing to be seen but the hand which acted as scribe. What impressed us boys more than anything else was the rumor that he had suffered his beard to grow, — such an anti-Sheffieldism being almost unheard of in those days, and the peculiar ornament of man being associated in our minds with nothing more recent than the patriarchs and apostles, whose effigies we were obliged to solace ourselves with weekly in the Family Bible. He came out of his oysterhood at last, and I knew him well, a kind-hearted man, who gave annual sleigh-rides to the town-paupers, and supplied the poor children with school-books. His favorite topic of conversation was Eternity, and like many other worthy persons, he used to fancy that meaning was an affair of aggregation, and that he doubled the intensity of what he said by the sole aid of the multiplication-table. "Eternity!" he used to say, "it is not a day; it is not a year; it is not a hundred years; it is not a thousand years; it is not a million years; no, sir," (the *sir* being thrown in to recall wandering attention,) "it is not ten million years!" and so on, his enthusiasm becoming a mere frenzy when he got among his sextillions, till I sometimes wished he had continued in retirement. He used to sit at the open window during thunder-storms, and had a Grecian feeling about death by lightning. In a certain sense he had his desire, for he died suddenly, — not by fire from heaven, but by the red flash of apoplexy, leaving his whole estate to charitable uses.

If K. were out of place as President, that was not P. as Greek Professor. Who that ever saw him can forget him, in his old age, like a lusty winter, frosty but kindly, with great silver spectacles of the heroic period, such as scarce twelve noses of these degenerate days could bear? He was a natural celibate, not dwelling "like the fly in the heart of the apple," but like a lonely bee rather, absconding himself in Hymettian flowers, incapable of matrimony as a solitary palm-tree. There was, to be sure, a tradition of youthful disappointment, and a touching story which L. told me perhaps confirms it. When Mrs. —— died, a carriage with blinds drawn followed the funeral train at some distance, and, when the coffin had been lowered into the grave, drove hastily away to escape that saddest of earthly sounds, the first rattle of earth upon the lid. It was afterward known that the carriage held a single mourner, — our grim and undemonstrative Professor. Yet I cannot bring myself to suppose him susceptible to any tender passion after that single lapse in the immaturity of reason. He might have joined the Abderites in singing their mad chorus from the Andromeda; but it would have been in deference to the language merely, and with a silent protest against the sentiment. I fancy him arranging his scrupulous toilet, not for Amaryllis or Neæra, but, like Machiavelli, for the society of his beloved classics. His ears had needed no prophylactic wax to pass the Sirens' isle; nay, he would have kept them the wider open, studious of the dialect in which they sang, and perhaps triumphantly detecting the Æolic digamma in their lay. A thoroughly single man, single-minded, single-hearted, buttoning over his single heart a single-breasted surtout, and wearing always a hat of a single fashion, — did he in secret regard the dual number of his favorite language as a weakness? The son of an officer of distinction in the Revolutionary War, he mounted the pulpit with the erect port of a soldier, and carried his cane more in the fashion of a weapon than a staff, but with the point lowered, in token of surrender to the peaceful proprieties of his calling. Yet sometimes the martial instincts would burst the cerements of black coat and clerical neckcloth, as once, when the students had got into a fight upon the training-field, and the licentious soldiery, furious with rum, had driven them at point of bayonet to the College gates, and even threatened to lift their arms against the Muses' bower. Then, like Major Goffe at Deerfield, suddenly appeared the gray-haired P., all his father resurgent in him, and shouted : " Now, my lads, stand your ground, you 're in the right now! Don't let one of them set foot within the College grounds!" Thus he allowed arms to get the better of the *toga;* but raised it, like the Prophet's breeches, into a banner, and carefully ushered resistance with a preamble of infringed right. Fidelity was his strong characteristic, and burned equally in him through a life of eighty-three years. He drilled himself till inflexible habit stood sentinel before all those postern-weaknesses which temperament leaves unbolted to temptation. A lover of the scholar's herb, yet loving freedom more, and knowing that the animal appetites ever hold one hand behind them for Satan to drop a bribe in, he would never have two cigars in his house at once, but walked every day to the shop to fetch his single diurnal solace. Nor would he trust himself with two on Saturdays, preferring (since he could not violate the Sabbath even by that infinitesimal traffic) to depend on Providential ravens, which were seldom wanting in the shape of some black-coated friend who knew his need, and honored the scruple that occasioned it. He was faithful, also, to his old hats, in which appeared the constant service of the antique world, and which he preserved forever, piled like a black pagoda under his dressing-table. No scarecrow was ever the residuary legatee of *his* beavers, though one of them in any of the neighboring peach-orchards would have been sovereign against an attack of Freshmen. He wore them all in turn, getting through all in the course of the year, like the sun through the signs of the zodiac, modulating them according to seasons and celestial phenomena, so that never was spider-web or chickweed so sensitive a weather-gauge as they. Nor did his political party find him less loyal. Taking all the tickets, he would seat himself apart, and carefully compare them with the list of regular nominations as printed in his Daily Advertiser, before he dropped his ballot in the box. In less ambitious moments, it almost seems to me that I would rather have had that slow, conscientious vote of P.'s alone, than to have been chosen Alderman of the Ward!

If you had walked to what was then Sweet Auburn by the pleasant Old Road, on some June morning thirty years ago, you would very likely have met two other characteristic persons, both phantasmagoric now, and belonging to the past. Fifty years earlier, the scarlet-coated, rapiered figures of Vassall, Lechmere, Oliver, and Brattle creaked up and down there on red-heeled shoes, lifting the ceremonious three-cornered hat, and offering the fugacious hospitalities of the snuff-box. They are all shadowy alike now, not one of your Etruscan Lucumos or Roman Consuls more so, my dear Storg. First is W., his *queue* slender and tapering, like the tail of a violet crab, held out horizontally by the high collar of his shepherd's-gray overcoat, whose style was of the latest when he studied at Leyden in his hot youth. The age of cheap clothes sees no more of those faithful old garments, as proper to their wearers and as distinctive as the barks of trees, and by long use interpenetrated with their very nature. Nor do we see so many Humors (still in the old sense) now that every man's soul belongs to the Public, as when social distinctions were more marked, and men felt that their personalities were their castles, in which they could intrench themselves against the world. Now-a-days men are shy of letting their true selves be seen, as if in some former life they had committed a crime, and were all the time afraid of discovery and arrest in this. Formerly they used to insist on your giving the wall to their peculiarities, and you may still find examples of it in the parson or the doctor of retired villages. One of W.'s oddities was touching. A little brook used to run across the street, and the sidewalk was carried over it by a broad stone. Of course there is no brook now. What use did that little glimpse of a ripple serve, where the children used to launch their chip fleets? W., in going over this stone, which gave a hollow resonance to the tread, had a trick of striking upon it three times with his cane, and muttering, "Tom, Tom, Tom!" I used to think he was only mimicking with his voice the sound of the blows, and possibly it was that sound which suggested his thought, for he was remembering a favorite nephew, prematurely dead. Perhaps Tom had sailed his boats there; perhaps the reverberation under the old man's foot hinted at the hollowness of life; perhaps the fleeting eddies of the water brought to mind the *fugaces an-*

nos. W., like P., wore amazing spectacles, fit to transmit no smaller image than the page of mightiest folios of Dioscorides or Hercules de Saxonia, and rising full-disked upon the beholder like those prodigies of two moons at once, portending change to monarchs. The great collar disallowing any independent rotation of the head, I remember he used to turn his whole person in order to bring their *foci* to bear upon an object. One can fancy that terrified Nature would have yielded up her secrets at once, without cross-examination, at their first glare. Through them he had gazed fondly into the great mare's-nest of Junius, publishing his observations upon the eggs found therein in a tall octavo. It was he who introduced vaccination to this Western World. Malicious persons disputing his claim to this distinction, he published this advertisement: "Lost, a gold snuff-box, with the inscription, 'The Jenner of the Old World to the Jenner of the New.' Whoever shall return the same to Dr. —— shall be suitably rewarded." It was never returned. Would the search after it have been as fruitless as that of the alchemist after his equally imaginary gold? Malicious persons persisted in believing the box as visionary as the claim it was meant to buttress with a semblance of reality. He used to stop and say good morning kindly, and pat the shoulder of the blushing school-boy who now, with the fierce snow-storm wildering without, sits and remembers sadly those old meetings and partings in the June sunshine.

Then there was S., whose resounding "Haw, haw, haw! by George!" positively enlarged the income of every dweller in Cambridge. In downright, honest good cheer and good neighborhood, it was worth five hundred a year to every one of us. Its jovial thunders cleared the mental air of every sulky cloud. Perpetual childhood dwelt in him, the childhood of his native Southern France, and its fixed air was all the time bubbling up and sparkling and winking in his eyes. It seemed as if his placid old face were only a mask behind which a merry Cupid had ambushed himself, peeping out all the while, and ready to drop it when the play grew tiresome. Every word he uttered seemed to be hilarious, no matter what the occasion. If he were sick, and you visited him, if he had met with a misfortune, (and there are few men so wise that they can look even at the back of a retiring sorrow with composure,) it was all one; his great laugh went off as if it were set like an alarm-clock, to run down, whether he would or no, at a certain nick. Even after an ordinary *Good morning!* (especially if to an old pupil, and in French,) the wonderful *Haw, haw, haw! by George!* would burst upon you unexpectedly, like a salute of artillery on some holiday which you had forgotten. Everything was a joke to him, — that the oath of allegiance had been administered to him by your grandfather, — that he had taught Prescott his first Spanish (of which he was proud), — no matter what. Everything came to him marked by Nature *Right side up, with care*, and he kept it so. The world to him, as to all of us, was like a medal, on the obverse of which is stamped the image of Joy, and on the reverse that of Care. S. never took the foolish pains to look at that other side, even if he knew its existence; much less would it have occurred to him to turn it into view, and insist that his friends should look at it with him. Nor was this a mere outside good-humor; its source was deeper, in a true Christian kindliness and amenity. Once, when he had been knocked down by a tipsily-driven sleigh, and was urged to prosecute the offenders, "No, no," he said, his wounds still fresh, "young blood! young blood! it must have its way; I was young myself." *Was!* few men come into life so young as S. went out. He landed in Boston (then the front door of America) in '93, and, in honor of the ceremony, had his head powdered afresh, and put on a suit of court-mourning before he set foot on the wharf. My fancy always dressed him in that violet silk, and his soul certainly wore a full court-suit. What was there ever like his bow? It was as if you had received a decoration, and could write yourself gentleman from that day forth. His hat rose, regreeting your own, and, having sailed through the stately curve of the old *régime*, sank gently back over that placid brain, which harbored no thought less white than the powder which covered it. I have sometimes imagined that there was a graduated arc over his head, invisible to other eyes than his, by which he meted out to each his rightful share of castorial consideration. I carry in my memory three exemplary bows. The first is that of an old beggar, who, already carrying in his hand a white hat, the gift of benevolence, took off the black one from his head also, and profoundly saluted me with both at once, giving me, in return for my alms, a dual benediction, puzzling as a nod from Janus Bifrons. The second I received from an old Cardinal, who was taking his walk just outside the Porta San

Giovanni at Rome. I paid him the courtesy due to his age and rank. Forthwith rose, first, *the* Hat; second, the hat of his confessor; third, that of another priest who attended him; fourth, the fringed cocked-hat of his coachman; fifth and sixth, the ditto, ditto, of his two footmen. Here was an investment, indeed; six hundred per cent interest on a single bow! The third bow, worthy to be noted in one's almanac among the other *mirabilia*, was that of S., in which courtesy had mounted to the last round of her ladder, — and tried to draw it up after her.

But the genial veteran is gone even while I am writing this, and I will play Old Mortality no longer. Wandering among these recent graves, my dear friend, we may chance upon ———; but no, I will not end my sentence. I bid you heartily farewell!

A MOOSEHEAD JOURNAL.

ADDRESSED TO THE EDELMANN STORG AT THE BAGNI DI LUCCA.

THURSDAY, 11*th August*.—I knew as little yesterday of the interior of Maine as the least penetrating person knows of the inside of that great social millstone which, driven by the river Time, sets imperatively agoing the several wheels of our individual activities. Born while Maine was still a province of native Massachusetts, I was as much a foreigner to it as yourself, my dear Storg. I had seen many lakes, ranging from that of Virgil's Cumæan to that of Scott's Caledonian Lady; but Moosehead, within two days of me, had never enjoyed the profit of being mirrored in my retina. At the sound of the name, no reminiscential atoms (according to Kenelm Digby's Theory of Association, — as good as any) stirred and marshalled themselves in my brain. The truth is, we think lightly of Nature's penny shows, and estimate what we see by the cost of the ticket. Empedocles gave his life for a pit-entrance to Ætna, and no doubt found his account in it. Accordingly, the clean face of Cousin Bull is imaged patronizingly in Lake George, and Loch Lomond glasses the hurried countenance of Jonathan, diving deeper in the streams of European association (and coming up drier) than any other man. Or is the cause of our not caring to see what is equally within the reach of all our neighbors to be sought in that aristocratic principle so deeply implanted in human nature? I knew a pauper graduate who always borrowed a black coat, and came to eat the Commencement dinner, — not that it was better than the one which daily graced the board of the public institution in which he hibernated (so to speak) during the other three hundred and sixty-four days of the year, save in this one particular, that none of his eleemosynary fellow-commoners could eat it. If there are unhappy men who wish that they were as the Babe Unborn, there are more who would aspire to the lonely distinction of being that other figurative personage, the Oldest Inhabitant. You remember the charming irresolution of our dear Esthwaite, (like Macheath between his two doxies,) divided between his theory that he is under thirty, and his pride at being the only one of us who witnessed the September gale and the rejoicings at the Peace? Nineteen years ago I was walking through the Franconia Notch, and stopped to chat with a hermit, who fed with gradual logs the unwearied teeth of a saw-mill. As the panting steel slit off the *slabs* of the log, so did the less willing machine of talk, acquiring a steadier up-and-down motion, pare away that outward bark of conversation which protects the core, and which, like other bark, has naturally most to do with the weather, the season, and the heat of the day. At length I asked him the best point of view for the Old Man of the Mountain.

" Dunno, — never see it."

Too young and too happy either to feel or affect the Juvenalian indifference, I was sincerely astonished, and I expressed it.

The log-compelling man attempted no justification, but after a little asked, " Come from Bawsn ? "

" Yes " (with peninsular pride).

" Goodle to see in the vycinity o' Bawsn."

" O yes ! " I said, and I thought, — see Boston and die ! see the State-Houses, old and new, the caterpillar wooden bridges crawling with innumerable legs across the flats of Charles ; see the Common, — largest park, doubtless, in the world, — with its files of trees planted as if by a drill-sergeant, and then for your *nunc dimittis!*

" I should like, 'awl, I *should* like to stan on Bunker Hill. You 've ben there offen, likely ? "

"N—o—o," unwillingly, seeing the little end of the horn in clear vision at the terminus of this Socratic perspective.

"'Awl, my young frien', you've larned neow thet wut a man *kin* see any day for nawthin', childern half price, he never doos see. Nawthin' pay, nawthin' vally."

With this modern instance of a wise saw, I departed, deeply revolving these things with myself, and convinced that, whatever the ratio of population, the average amount of human nature to the square mile is the same the world over. I thought of it when I saw people upon the Pincian wondering at the Alchemist sun, as if he never burned the leaden clouds to gold in sight of Charles Street. I thought of it when I found eyes first discovering at Mont Blanc how beautiful snow was. As I walked on, I said to myself, There is one exception, wise hermit,—it is just these *gratis* pictures which the poet puts in his show-box, and which we all gladly pay Wordsworth and the rest for a peep at. The divine faculty is to see what everybody can look at.

While every well-informed man in Europe, from the barber down to the diplomatist, has his view of the Eastern Question, why should I not go personally down East and see for myself? Why not, like Tancred, attempt my own solution of the Mystery of the Orient, — doubly mysterious when you begin the two words with capitals? You know my way of doing things, to let them simmer in my mind gently for months, and at last do them *impromptu* in a kind of desperation, driven by the Eumenides of unfulfilled purpose. So, after talking about Moosehead till nobody believed me capable of going thither, I found myself at the Eastern Railway station. The only event of the journey hither (I am now at Waterville) was a boy hawking exhilaratingly the last great railroad smash, — thirteen lives lost, — and no doubt devoutly wishing there had been fifty. This having a mercantile interest in horrors, holding stock, as it were, in murder, misfortune, and pestilence, must have an odd effect on the human mind. The birds of ill-omen, at whose sombre flight the rest of the world turn pale, are the ravens which bring food to this little outcast in the wilderness. If this lad give thanks for daily bread, it would be curious to inquire what that phrase represents to his understanding. If there ever be a plum in it, it is Sin or Death that puts it in. Other details of my dreadful ride I will spare you. Suffice it that I arrived here in safety, — in complexion like an Ethiopian serenader half got-up, and so broiled and peppered that I was more like a devilled kidney than anything else I can think of.

10 P. M. — The civil landlord and neat chamber at the "Elmwood House" were very grateful, and after tea I set forth to explore the town. It has a good chance of being pretty; but, like most American towns, it is in a hobbledehoy age, growing yet, and one cannot tell what may happen. A child with

great promise of beauty is often spoiled by its second teeth. There is something agreeable in the sense of completeness which a walled town gives one. It is entire, like a crystal,— a work which man has succeeded in finishing. I think the human mind pines more or less where everything is new, and is better for a diet of stale bread. The number of Americans who visit the Old World is beginning to afford matter of speculation to observant Europeans, and the deep inspirations with which they breathe the air of antiquity, as if their mental lungs had been starved with too thin an atmosphere. For my own part, I never saw a house which I thought old enough to be torn down. It is too like that Scythian fashion of knocking old people on the head. I cannot help thinking that the indefinable something which we call *character* is cumulative,— that the influence of the same climate, scenery, and associations for several generations is necessary to its gathering head, and that the process is disturbed by con annual change of place. The American is nomadic in religion, in ideas, in morals, and leaves his faith and opinions with as much indifference as the house in which he was born. However, we need not bother: Nature takes care not to leave out of the great heart of society either of its two ventricles of hold-back and go-ahead.

It seems as if every considerable American town must have its one specimen of everything, and so there is a college in Waterville, the buildings of which are three in number, of brick, and quite up to the average ugliness which seems essential in edifices of this description. Unhappily, they do not reach that extreme of ugliness where it and beauty come together in the clasp of fascination. We erect handsomer factories for cottons, woollens, and steam-engines, than for doctors, lawyers, and parsons. The truth is, that, till our struggle with nature is over, till this shaggy hemisphere is tamed and subjugated, the workshop will be the college whose degrees will be most valued. Moreover, steam has made travel so easy that the great university of the world is open to all comers, and the old cloister system is falling astern. Perhaps it is only the more needed, and, were I rich, I should like to found a few lazyships in my Alma Mater as a kind of counterpoise. The Anglo-Saxon race has accepted the primal curse as a blessing, has deified work, and would not have thanked Adam for abstaining from the apple. They would have dammed the four rivers of Paradise, substituted cotton for fig-leaves among the antediluvian populations, and commended man's first disobedience as a wise measure of political economy. But to return to our college. We cannot have fine buildings till we are less in a hurry. We snatch an education like a meal at a railroad-station. Just in time to make us dyspeptic, the whistle shrieks, and we must rush, or lose our places in the great train of life. Yet noble architecture is one element of patriotism, and an eminent one of culture, the finer portions of which are taken in by unconscious absorption through the pores of the mind from the surrounding atmosphere. I suppose we must wait, for we are a great bivouac as yet rather than a nation, — on the march from the Atlantic to the Pacific, — and pitch tents instead of building houses. Our very villages seem to be in motion, following westward the bewitching music of some Pied Piper of Hamelin. We still feel the great push toward sundown given to the peoples somewhere in the gray dawn of history. The cliff-swallow alone of all animated nature emigrates eastward.

Friday, 12*th*. — The coach leaves Waterville at five o'clock in the morning, and one must breakfast in the dark at a quarter past four, because a train starts at twenty minutes before five, — the passengers by both conveyances being pastured gregariously. So one must be up at half past three. The primary geological formations contain no trace of man, and it seems to me that these eocene periods of the day are not fitted for sustaining the human forms of life. One of the Fathers held that the sun was created to be worshipped at his rising by the Gentiles. The more reason that Christians (except, perhaps, early Christians) should abstain from these heathenish ceremonials. As one arriving by an early train is welcomed by a drowsy maid with the sleep scarce brushed out of her hair, and finds empty grates and polished mahogany, on whose arid plains the pioneers of breakfast have not yet encamped, so a person waked thus unseasonably is sent into the world before his faculties are up and dressed to serve him. It might have been for this reason that my stomach resented for several hours a piece of fried beefsteak which I forced upon it, or, more properly speaking, a piece of that leathern conveniency which in these regions assumes the name. You will find it as hard to believe, my dear Storg, as that quarrel of the Sorbonists, whether one should say *ego amat* or no, that the use of the gridiron is unknown hereabout, and so near a river named after St. Lawrence, too!

To-day has been the hottest day of the season, yet our drive has not been unpleasant. For a considerable distance we followed the course of the Sebasticook River, a pretty stream with alternations of dark brown pools and wine-colored rapids. On each side of the road the land had been cleared, and little one-story farm-houses were scattered at intervals. But the stumps still held out in most of the fields, and the tangled wilderness closed in behind, striped here and there with the slim white trunks of the elm. As yet only the edges of the great forest have been nibbled away. Sometimes a root-fence stretched up its bleaching antlers, like the trophies of a giant hunter. Now and then the houses thickened into an unsocial-looking village, and we drove up to the grocery to leave and take a mail-bag, stopping again presently to water the horses at some pallid little tavern, whose one red-curtained eye (the bar-room) had been put out by the inexorable thrust of Maine Law. Had Shenstone travelled this road, he would never have written that famous stanza of his; had Johnson, he would never have quoted it. They are to real inns as the skull of Yorick to his face. Where these villages occurred at a distance from the river, it was difficult to account for them. On the riverbank, a saw-mill or a tannery served as a logical premise, and saved them from total inconsequentiality. As we trailed along, at the rate of about four miles an hour, it was discovered that one of our mail-bags was missing. "Guess somebody 'll pick it up," said the driver coolly; "'t any rate, likely there's nothin' in it." Who knows how long it took some Elam D. or Zebulon K. to compose the missive intrusted to that vagrant bag, and how much longer to persuade Pamela Grace or Sophronia Melissa that it had really and truly been written? The discovery of our loss was made by a tall man who sat next to me on the top of the coach, every one of whose senses seemed to be prosecuting its several investigation as we went along. Presently, sniffing gently, he remarked: "'Pears to me 's though I smelt sunthin'. Ain't the *aix het*, think?" The driver pulled up, and, sure enough, the off fore-wheel was found to be smoking. In three minutes he had snatched a rail from the fence, made a lever, raised the coach, and taken off the wheel, bathing the hot axle and box with water from the river. It was a pretty spot, and I was not sorry to lie under a beech-tree (Tityrus-like, meditating over my pipe) and watch the operations of the fire-annihilator. I could not help contrasting the ready helpfulness of our driver, all of whose wits were about him, current, and redeemable in the specie of action on emergency, with an incident of travel in Italy, where, under a somewhat similar stress of circumstances, our *vetturino* had nothing for it but to dash his hat on the ground and call on Sant' Antonio, the Italian Hercules.

There being four passengers for the Lake, a vehicle called a mud-wagon was detailed at Newport for our accommodation. In this we jolted and rattled along at a livelier pace than in the coach. As we got farther north, the country (especially the hills) gave evidence of longer cultivation. About the thriving town of Dexter we saw fine farms and crops. The houses, too, became prettier; hop-vines were trained about the doors, and hung their clustering thyrsi over the open windows. A kind of wild rose (called by the country folk the primrose) and asters were planted about the door-yards, and orchards, commonly of natural fruit, added to the pleasant home-look. But everywhere we could see that the war between the white man and the forest was still fierce, and that it would be a long while yet before the axe was buried. The haying being over, fires blazed or smouldered against the stumps in the fields, and the blue smoke widened slowly upward through the quiet August atmosphere. It seemed to me that I could hear a sigh now and then from the immemorial pines, as they stood watching these camp-fires of the inexorable invader. Evening set in, and, as we crunched and crawled up the long gravelly hills, I sometimes began to fancy that Nature had forgotten to make the corresponding descent on the other side. But erelong we were rushing down at full speed; and, inspired by the dactylic beat of the horses' hoofs, I essayed to repeat the opening lines of Evangeline. At the moment I was beginning, we plunged into a hollow, where the soft clay had been overcome by a road of unhewn logs. I got through one line to this corduroy accompaniment, somewhat as a country choir stretches a short metre on the Procrustean rack of a long-drawn tune. The result was like this: —

" Thihis ihis thebe fohorest prihihimeheval ; thehe murhur-muring pihines hahand thebe hehemlohocks ! "

At a quarter past eleven, P. M., we reached Greenville, (a little village which looks as if it had dripped down from the hills, and settled in the hollow at the foot of the lake,) having accomplished seventy-two miles in eighteen hours. The tavern was totally extinguished. The driver rapped upon the bar-room window, and after a while we saw heat-lightnings of unsuccessful matches followed by a low grumble of vocal thunder, which I am afraid took the form of imprecation. Presently there was a great success, and the steady blur of lighted tallow succeeded the fugitive brilliance of the pine. A hostler fumbled the door open, and stood staring at but not seeing us, with the sleep sticking out all over him. We at last contrived to launch him, more like an insensible missile than an intelligent or intelligible being, at the slumbering landlord, who came out wide-awake, and welcomed us as so many half-dollars, — twenty-five cents each for bed, *ditto* breakfast. O Shenstone, Shenstone! The only roost was in the garret, which had been made into a single room, and contained eleven double-beds, ranged along the walls. It was like sleeping in a hospital. However, nice customs curtsy to eighteen-hour rides, and we slept.

Saturday, 13th. — This morning I performed my toilet in the bar-room, where there was an abundant supply of water, and a halo of interested spectators. After a sufficient breakfast, we embarked on the little steamer Moosehead, and were soon throbbing up the lake. The boat, it appeared, had been chartered by a party, this not being one of her regular trips. Accordingly we were mulcted in twice the usual fee, the philosophy of which I could not understand. However, it always comes easier to us to comprehend why we receive than why we pay. I dare say it was quite clear to the captain. There were three or four clearings on the western shore; but after passing these, the lake became wholly primeval, and looked to us as it did to the first adventurous Frenchman who paddled across it. Sometimes a cleared point would be pink with the blossoming willow-herb, "a cheap and excellent substitute" for heather, and, like all such, not *quite* so good as the real thing. On all sides rose deep-blue mountains, of remarkably graceful outline, and more fortunate than common in their names. There were the Big and Little Squaw, the Spencer and Lily-bay Mountains. It was debated whether we saw Katahdin or not, (perhaps more useful as an intellectual exercise than the assured vision would have been,) and presently Mount Kineo rose abruptly before us, in shape not unlike the island of Capri. Mountains are called great natural features, and why they should not retain their names long enough for them also to become naturalized, it is hard to say. Why should every new surveyor rechristen them with the gubernatorial patronymics of the current year? They are geological noses, and, as they are aquiline or pug, indicate terrestrial idiosyncrasies. A cosmical physiognomist, after a glance at them, will draw no vague inference as to the character of the country. The word *nose* is no better than any other word; but since the organ has got that name, it is convenient to keep it. Suppose we had to label our facial prominences every season with the name of our provincial governor, how should *we* like it? If the old names have no other meaning, they have that of age; and, after all, meaning is a plant of slow growth, as every reader of Shakespeare knows. It is well enough to call mountains after their discoverers, for Nature has a knack of throwing doublets, and somehow contrives it that discoverers have good names. Pike's Peak is a curious hit in this way. But these surveyors' names have no natural *stick* in them. They remind one of the epithets of poetasters, which peel off like a badly gummed postage-stamp. The early settlers did better, and there is something pleasant in the sound of Graylock, Saddleback, and Great Haystack.

> "I love those names
> Wherewith the exiled farmer tames
> Nature down to companionship
>   With his old world's more homely mood,
> And strives the shaggy wild to clip
>   With arms of familiar habitude."

It is possible that Mount Marcy and Mount Hitchcock may sound as well hereafter as Hellespont and Peloponnesus, when the heroes, their namesakes, have become mythic with antiquity. But that is to look forward a great way. I am no fanatic for Indian nomenclature, — the name of my native district having been Pigsgusset, — but let us at least agree on names for ten years.

There were a couple of loggers on board, in red flannel shirts, and with rifles. They were the first I had seen, and I was interested in their appearance. They were tall, well-knit men, straight as Robin Hood, and with a quiet, self-contained look that pleased me. I fell into talk with one of them.

"Is there a good market for the farmers here in the woods?" I asked.

"None better. They can sell what they raise at their doors, and for the best of prices. The lumberers want it all, and more."

"It must be a lonely life. But then we all have to pay more or less life for a living."

"Well, it *is* lonesome. Shouldn't like it. After all, the best crop a man can raise is a good crop of society. We don't live none too long, anyhow; and without society a fellow could n't tell more 'n half the time whether he was alive or not."

This speech gave me a glimpse into the life of the lumberers' camp. It was plain that there a man would soon find out how much alive he was, — there he could learn to estimate his quality, weighed in the nicest self-adjusting balance. The best arm at the axe or the paddle, the surest eye for a road or for the weak point of a *jam*, the steadiest foot upon the squirming log, the most persuasive voice to the tugging oxen, — all these things are rapidly settled, and so an aristocracy is evolved from this democracy of the woods, for good old mother Nature speaks Saxon still, and with her either Canning or Kenning means King.

A string of five loons was flying back and forth in long, irregular zigzags, uttering at intervals their wild, tremulous cry, which always seems far away, like the last faint pulse of echo dying among the hills, and which is one of those few sounds that, instead of disturbing solitude, only deepen and confirm it. On our inland ponds they are usually seen in pairs, and I asked if it were common to meet five together. My question was answered by a queer-looking old man, chiefly remarkable for a pair of enormous cowhide boots, over which large blue trousers of frocking strove in vain to crowd themselves.

"Wahl, 't ain't ushil," said he, "and it's called a sign o' rain comin', that is."

"Do you think it will rain?"

With the caution of a veteran *auspex*, he evaded a direct reply. "Wahl, they *du* say it's a sign o' rain comin'," said he.

I discovered afterward that my interlocutor was Uncle Zeb. Formerly, every New England town had its representative uncle. He was not a pawnbroker, but some elderly man who, for want of more defined family ties, had gradually assumed this avuncular relation to the community, inhabiting the border-land between respectability and the almshouse, with no regular calling, but working at haying, wood-sawing, whitewashing, associated with the demise of pigs and the ailments of cattle, and possessing as much patriotism as might be implied in a devoted attachment to "New England" — with a good deal of sugar and very little water in it. Uncle Zeb was a good specimen of this palæozoic class, extinct among us for the most part, or surviving, like the Dodo, in the Botany Bays of society. He was ready to contribute (somewhat muddily) to all general conversation; but his chief topics were his boots and the 'Roostick war. Upon the lowlands and levels of ordinary palaver he would make rapid and unlooked-for incursions; but, provision failing, he would retreat to these two fastnesses, whence it was impossible to dislodge him, and to which he knew innumerable passes and short cuts quite beyond the conjecture of common woodcraft. His mind opened naturally to these two subjects, like a book to some favorite passage. As the ear accustoms itself to any sound recurring regularly, such as the ticking of a clock, and, without a conscious effort of attention, takes no impression from it whatever, so does the mind find a natural safeguard against this pendulum species of discourse, and performs its duties in the parliament by an unconscious reflex action, like the beating of the heart or the movement of the lungs. If talk seemed to be flagging, our Uncle would put the heel of one boot upon the toe of the other, to bring it within point-blank range, and say, " Wahl, I stump the Devil himself to make that 'ere boot hurt *my* foot," leaving us in doubt whether it were the virtue of the foot or its case which set at naught the wiles of the adversary; or, looking up suddenly, he would exclaim, " Wahl, we eat some beans to the 'Roostick war, I tell *you!*' " When his poor old clay was wet with **gin**, his thoughts and words acquired a rank flavor from it, as from too strong a fertilizer. At such times, too, his fancy commonly reverted to a pre-historic period of his life, when he singly had settled all the surrounding country, subdued the Injuns and other wild animals, and named all the towns.

We talked of the winter-camps and the life there. " The best thing is," said our Uncle, " to hear a log squeal thru the snow. Git a good, cole, frosty mornin', in Febuary say, an' take an' hitch the critters on to a log that 'll scale seven thousan', an' it 'll squeal as pooty as an'thin' *you* ever hearn, I tell *you.*"

A pause.

" Lessee, — seen Cal Hutchins lately ? "

" No."

" Seems to me 's though I hed n't seen Cal sence the 'Roostick war. Wahl," &c., &c.

Another pause.

" To look at them boots you 'd think they was too large; but kind o' git your foot into 'em, and they're as easy 's a glove." (I observed that he never seemed really to get his foot in, — there was always a qualifying *kind o'*.) "Wahl, my foot can play in 'em like a young hedgehog."

By this time we had arrived at Kineo, — a flourishing village of one house, the tavern kept by 'Squire Barrows. The 'Squire is a large, hearty man, with a voice as clear and strong as a northwest wind, and a great laugh suitable to it. His table is neat and well supplied, and he waits upon it himself in the good old landlordly fashion. One may be much better off here, to my thinking, than in one of those gigantic Columbaria which are foisted upon us patient Americans for hotels, and where one is packed away in a pigeon-hole so near the heavens that, if the comet should flirt its tail, (no unlikely thing in the month of flies,) one would be in danger of being brushed away. Here one does not pay his diurnal three dollars for an undivided five-hundredth part of the pleasure of looking at gilt gingerbread. Here one's relations are with the monarch himself, and one is not obliged to wait the slow leisure of those "attentive clerks" whose praises are sung by thankful deadheads, and to whom the slave who pays may feel as much gratitude as might thrill the heart of a brown-paper parcel toward the express-man who labels it and chucks it under his counter.

Sunday, 14th. — The loons were right. About midnight it began to rain in earnest, and did not hold up till about ten o'clock this morning. "This is a Maine dew," said a shaggy woodman cheerily, as he shook the water out of his wide-awake, "if it don't look out sharp, it 'll begin to rain afore it thinks on 't." The day was mostly spent within doors; but I found good and intelligent society. We should have to be shipwrecked on Juan Fernandez not to find men who knew more than we. In these travelling encounters one is thrown upon his own resources, and is worth just what he carries about him. The social currency of home, the smooth-worn coin which passes freely among friends and neighbors, is of no account. We are thrown back upon the old system of barter; and, even with savages, we bring away only as much of the wild wealth of the woods as we carry beads of thought and experience, strung one by one in painful years, to pay for them with. A useful old jackknife will buy more than the daintiest Louis Quinze paper-folder fresh from Paris. Perhaps the kind of intelligence one gets in these out-of-the-way places is the best, — where one takes a fresh man after breakfast instead of the damp morning paper, and where the magnetic telegraph of human sympathy flashes swift news from brain to brain.

Meanwhile, at a pinch, to-morrow's weather can be discussed. The augury from the flight of birds is favorable, — the loons no longer prophesying rain. The wind also is hauling round to the right quarter, according to some, to the wrong, if we are to believe others.

Each man has his private barometer of hope, the mercury in which is more or less sensitive, and the opinion vibrant with its rise or fall. Mine has an index which can be moved mechanically. I fixed it at *set fair*, and resigned myself. I read an old volume of the Patent-Office Report on Agriculture, and stored away a beautiful pile of facts and observations for future use, which the current of occupation, at its first freshet, would sweep quietly off to blank oblivion. Practical application is the only mordant which will set things in the memory. Study, without it, is gymnastics, and not work, which alone will get intellectual bread. One learns more metaphysics from a single temptation than from all the philosophers. It is curious, though, how tyrannical the habit of reading is, and what shifts we make to escape thinking. There is no bore we dread being left alone with so much as our own minds. I have seen a sensible man study a stale newspaper in a country tavern, and husband it as he would an old shoe on a raft after shipwreck. Why not try a bit of hibernation? There are few brains that would not be better for living on their own fat a little while. With these reflections, I, notwithstanding, spent the afternoon over my Report. If our own experience is of so little use to us, what a dolt is he who recommends to man or nation the experience of others! Like the mantle in the old ballad, it is always too short or too long, and exposes or trips us up. "Keep out of that candle," says old Father Miller, "or you'll get a singeing." "Pooh, pooh, father, I've been dipped in the new asbestos preparation," and *frozz!* it is all over with young Hopeful. How many warnings have been drawn from Pretorian bands, and Janizaries, and Mamelukes, to make Napoleon III. impossible in 1851! I found myself thinking the same thoughts over again, when we walked later on the beach and picked up pebbles. The old time-ocean throws upon its shores just such rounded and polished results of the eternal turmoil, but we only see the beauty of those we have got the headache in stooping for ourselves, and wonder at the dull brown bits of common stone with which our comrades have stuffed their pockets. Afterwards this little fable came of it.

DOCTOR LOBSTER.

A PERCH, who had the toothache, once
Thus moaned, like any human dunce :
" Why must great souls exhaust so soon
Life's thin and unsubstantial boon ?
Existence on such sculpin terms, —
Their vulgar loves and hard-won worms,—
What is it all but dross to me,
Whose nature craves a larger sea ;
Whose inches, six from head to tail,
Enclose the spirit of a whale ;
Who, if great baits were still to win,
By watchful eye and fearless fin
Might with the Zodiac's awful twain
Room for a third immortal gain ?
Better the crowd's unthinking plan, —
The hook, the jerk, the frying-pan !
O Death, thou ever roaming shark,
Ingulf me in eternal dark ! "

The speech was cut in two by flight :
A real shark had come in sight ;

No metaphoric monster, one
It soothes despair to call upon,
But stealthy, sidelong, grim, I wis,
A bit of downright Nemesis;
While it recovered from the shock,
Our fish took shelter 'neath a rock:
This was an ancient lobster's house,
A lobster of prodigious *nous*,
So old that barnacles had spread
Their white encampments o'er its head,
And of experience so stupend,
His claws were blunted at the end,
Turning life's iron pages o'er,
That shut and can be oped no more.

Stretching a hospitable claw,
"At once," said he, "the point I saw;
My dear young friend, your case I rue,
Your great-great-grandfather I knew;
He was a tried and tender friend
I know, — I ate him in the end:
In this vile sea a pilgrim long,
Still my sight's good, my memory strong;
The only sign that age is near
Is a slight deafness in this ear;
I understand your case as well
As this my old familiar shell;
This sorrow's a new-fangled notion,
Come in since first I knew the ocean;

We had no radicals, nor crimes,
Nor lobster-pots, in good old times;
Your traps and nets and hooks we owe
To Messieurs Louis Blanc and Co.;
I say to all my sons and daughters,
Shun Red Republican hot waters;
No lobster ever cast his lot
Among the reds, but went to pot:
Your trouble 's in the jaw, you said?
Come, let me just nip off your head,
And, when a new one comes, the pain
Will never trouble you again:
Nay, nay, fear naught: 't is nature's law.
Four times I 've lost this starboard claw;
And still, erelong, another grew,
Good as the old, — and better too!"

The perch consented, and next day
An osprey, marketing that way,
Picked up a fish without a head,
Floating with belly up, stone dead.

MORAL.

Sharp are the teeth of ancient saws,
And sauce for goose is gander's sauce;
But perch's heads are n't lobster's claws.

Monday, 15*th*. — The morning was fine, and we were called at four o'clock. At the moment my door was knocked at, I was mounting a giraffe with that charming *nil admirari* which characterizes dreams, to visit Prester John. *Rat-tat-tat-tat!* upon my door and upon the horn gate of dreams also. I remarked to my skowhegan (the Tâtar for giraffe-driver) that I was quite sure the animal had the *raps*, a common disease among them, for I heard a queer knocking noise inside him. It is the sound of his joints, O Tambourgi! (an Oriental term of reverence,) and proves him to be of the race of El Keirat. *Rat-tat-tat-too!* and I lost my dinner at the Prester's, embarking for a voyage to the Northwest Carry instead. Never use the word *canoe*, my dear Storg, if you wish to retain your self-respect. *Birch* is the term among us backwoodsmen. I never knew it till yesterday; but, like a true philosopher, I made it appear as if I had been intimate with it from childhood. The rapidity with which the human mind levels itself to the standard around it gives us the most pertinent warning as to the company we keep. It is as hard for most characters to stay at their own average point in all companies, as for a thermometer to say 65° for twenty-four hours together. I like this in our friend Johannes Taurus, that he carries everywhere and maintains his insular temperature, and will have everything accommodate itself to that. Shall I confess that this morning I would rather have broken the moral law, than have endangered the equipoise of the birch by my awkwardness? that I should have been prouder of a compliment to my paddling, than to have had both my guides suppose me the author of Hamlet? Well, Cardinal Richelieu used to jump over chairs.

We were to paddle about twenty miles, but we made it rather more by crossing and recrossing the lake. Twice we landed, — once at a camp, where we found the cook alone, baking bread and gingerbread. Monsieur Soyer would have been startled a little by this shaggy professor, — this Pre-Raphaelite of cookery. He represented the *salæratus* period of the art, and his bread was of a brilliant yellow, like those cakes tinged with saffron, which hold out so long against time and the flies in little water-side shops of seaport towns,—dingy extremities of trade fit to moulder on Lethe wharf. His water was better, squeezed out of ice-cold granite in the neighboring mountains, and sent through subterranean ducts to sparkle up by the door of the camp.

"There's nothin' so sweet an' hulsome as your *real* spring water," said Uncle Zeb, "git it pure. But it's dreffle hard to git it that ain't got sunthin' the matter of it. Snow-water 'll burn a man's inside out,—I larned that to the 'Roostick war,—and the snow lays terrible long on some o' thes'ere hills. Me an' Eb Stiles was up old Ktahdn once jest about this time o' year, an' we come acrost a kind o' holler like, as full o' snow as your stockin's full o' your foot. *I* see it fust, an' took an' rammed a settin'-pole wahl, it was all o' twenty foot into 't, an' could n't fin' no bottom. I dunno as there's snow-water enough in this to do no hurt. I don't somehow seem to think that *real* spring-water's so plenty as it used to be." And Uncle Zeb, with perhaps a little over-refinement of scrupulosity, applied his lips to the Ethiop ones of a bottle of raw gin, with a kiss that drew out its very soul, — a *basia* that Secundus might have sung. He must have been a wonderful judge of water, for he analyzed this, and detected its latent snow simply by his eye, and without the clumsy process of tasting. I could not help thinking that he had made the desert his dwelling-place chiefly in order to enjoy the ministrations of this one fair spirit unmolested.

We pushed on. Little islands loomed trembling between sky and water, like hanging gardens. Gradually the filmy trees defined themselves, the aerial enchantment lost its potency, and we came up with common prose islands that had so late been magical and poetic. The old story of the attained and unattained. About noon we reached the head of the lake, and took possession of a deserted *wongen*, in which to cook and eat our dinner. No Jew, I am sure, can have a more thorough dislike of salt pork than I have in a normal state, yet I had already eaten it raw with hard bread for lunch, and relished it keenly. We soon had our tea-kettle over the fire, and before long the cover was chattering with the escaping steam, which had thus vainly begged of all men to be saddled and bridled, till James Watt one day happened to overhear it. One of our guides shot three Canada grouse, and these were turned slowly between the fire and a bit of salt pork, which dropped fatness upon them as it fried. Although *my* fingers were certainly not made before knives and forks, yet they served as a convenient substitute for those more ancient inventions. We sat round, Turk-fashion, and ate thankfully, while a party of aborigines of the Mosquito tribe, who had camped in the *wongen* before we arrived, dined upon us. I do not know what the British Protectorate of the Mosquitoes amounts to; but, as I squatted there at the mercy of these blood-thirsty savages, I no longer wondered that the classic Everett had been stung into a willingness for war on the question.

"This 'ere 'd be about a complete place for a camp, ef there was on'y a spring o' sweet water handy. Frizzled pork goes wal, don't it? Yes, an' sets wal, too," said Uncle Zeb, and he again tilted his bottle, which rose nearer and nearer to an angle of forty-five at every gurgle. He then broached a curious dietetic theory: "The reason we take salt pork along is cos it packs handy: you git the greatest amount o' board in the smallest compass, — let alone that it's more nourishin' than an'thin' else. It kind o' don't disgest so quick, but stays by ye, anourishin' ye all the while.

"A feller can live wal on frizzled pork an' good spring-water, git it *good*. To the 'Roostick war we did n't ask for nothin' better, — on'y beans." (*Tilt, tilt, gurgle, gurgle.*) Then, with an apparent feeling of inconsistency, "But then, come to git used to a particular *kind* o' spring-water, an' it makes a feller hard to suit. Most all sorts o' water taste kind o' *in*sipid away from home. Now, I 've gut a spring to my place that 's as sweet — wahl, it 's as sweet as maple sap. A feller acts about water jest as he does about a pair o' boots. It 's all on it in gittin' wonted. Now, *them* boots," &c., &c. (*Gurgle, gurgle, gurgle, smack!*)

All this while he was packing away the remains of the pork and hard bread in two large firkins. This accomplished, we re-embarked, our uncle on his way to the birch essaying a kind of song in four or five parts, of which the words were hilarious and the tune profoundly melancholy, and which was finished, and the rest of his voice apparently jerked out of him in one sharp falsetto note by his tripping over the root of a tree. We paddled a short distance up a brook which came into the lake smoothly through a little meadow not far off. We soon reached the Northwest Carry, and our guide, pointing through the woods, said: "That's the Cannydy road. You can travel that clearn to Kebeck, a hunderd an' twenty mile," — a privilege of which I respectfully declined to avail myself. The offer, however, remains open to the public. The Carry is called two miles; but this is the estimate of somebody who had nothing to lug. I had a headache and all my baggage, which, with a traveller's instinct, I had brought with me. (P. S. — I did not even take the keys out of my pocket, and both my bags were wet through before I came back.) *My* estimate of the distance is eighteen thousand six hundred and seventy-four miles and three quarters, — the fraction being the part left to be travelled after one of my companions most kindly insisted on relieving me of my heaviest bag. I know very well that the ancient Roman soldiers used to carry sixty pounds' weight, and all that; but I am not, and never shall be, an ancient Roman soldier, — no, not even in the miraculous Thundering Legion. Uncle Zeb slung the two provender firkins across his shoulder, and trudged along, grumbling that " he never see sech a contrairy pair as them." He had begun upon a second bottle of his "particular kind o' spring-water," and, at every rest, the gurgle of this peripatetic fountain might be heard, followed by a smack, a fragment of mosaic song, or a confused clatter with the cowhide boots, being an arbitrary symbol, intended to represent the festive dance. Christian's pack gave him not half so much trouble as the firkins gave Uncle Zeb. It grew harder and harder to sling them, and with every fresh gulp of the Batavian elixir, they got heavier. Or rather, the truth was, that his hat grew heavier, in which he was carrying on an extensive manufacture of bricks without straw. At last affairs reached a crisis, and a particularly favorable pitch offering, with a puddle at the foot of it, even *the* boots afforded no sufficient ballast, and away went our uncle, the satellite firkins accompanying faithfully his headlong flight. Did ever exiled monarch or disgraced minister find the cause of his fall in himself? Is there not always a strawberry at the bottom of our cup of life, on which we can lay all the blame of our deviations from the straight path? Till now Uncle Zeb had contrived to give a gloss of volition to smaller stumblings and gyrations, by exaggerating them into an appearance of playful burlesque. But the present case was beyond any such subterfuges. He held a bed of justice where he sat, and then arose slowly, with a stern determination of vengeance stiffening every muscle of his face. But what would he select as the culprit? " It's that cussed firkin," he mumbled to himself. " I never knowed a firkin cair on so, — no, not in the 'Roostehicick war. There, go long, will ye? and don't come back till you 've larned how to walk with a genelman!" And, seizing the unhappy scapegoat by the bail, he hurled it into the forest. It is a curious circumstance, that it was not the firkin containing the bottle which was thus condemned to exile.

The end of the Carry was reached at last, and, as we drew near it, we heard a sound of shouting and laughter. It came from a party of men making hay of the wild grass in Seboomok meadows, which lie around Seboomok pond, into which the Carry empties itself. Their camp was near, and our two hunters set out for it, leaving us seated in the birch on the plashy border of the pond. The repose was perfect. Another heaven hallowed and deepened the polished lake, and through that nether world the fish-hawk's double floated with balanced wings, or, wheeling suddenly, flashed his whitened breast against the sun. As the clattering kingfisher flew unsteadily across, and seemed to push his heavy head along with ever-renewing effort, a visionary mate flitted from downward tree to tree below. Some tall alders shaded us from the sun, in whose yellow afternoon light the drowsy forest was steeped, giving out that wholesome resinous perfume, almost the only warm odor which it is refreshing to breathe. The tame hay-cocks in the midst of the wildness gave one a pleasant reminiscence of home, like hearing one's native tongue in a strange country.

Presently our hunters came back, bringing with them a tall, thin, active-looking man, with black eyes, that glanced unconsciously on all sides, like one of those spots of sunlight which a child dances up and down the street with a bit of looking-glass. This was M., the captain of the hay-makers, a famous river-driver, and who was to have fifty men under him next winter. I could now understand that sleepless vigilance of eye. He had consented to take two of our party in his birch to search for moose. A quick, nervous, decided man, he got them into the birch, and was off instantly, without a superfluous word.

He evidently looked upon them as he would upon a couple of logs which he was to deliver at a certain place. Indeed, I doubt if life and the world presented themselves to Napier himself in a more logarithmic way. His only thought was to do the immediate duty well, and to pilot his particular raft down the crooked stream of life to the ocean beyond. The birch seemed to feel him as an inspiring soul, and slid away straight and swift for the outlet of the pond. As he disappeared under the over-arching alders of the brook, our two hunters could not repress a grave and measured applause. There is never any extravagance among these woodmen; their eye, accustomed to reckoning the number of feet which a tree will *scale*, is rapid and close in its guess of the amount of stuff in a man. It was *laudari a laudato*, however, for they themselves were accounted good men in a birch. I was amused, in talking with them about him, to meet with an instance of that tendency of the human mind to assign some utterly improbable reason for gifts which seem unaccountable. After due praise, one of them said, "I guess he's got some Injun in him," although I knew very well that the speaker had a thorough contempt for the red-man, mentally and physically. Here was mythology in a small way, — the same that under more favorable auspices hatched Helen out of an egg and gave Merlin an Incubus for a father. I was pleased with all I saw of M. He was in his narrow sphere a true ἄναξ ἀνδρῶν, and the ragged edges of his old hat seemed to become coronated as I looked at him. He impressed me as a man really educated, — that is, with his aptitudes *drawn out* and ready for use. He was A. M. and LL. D. in Woods College, — Axe-master and Doctor of Logs. Are not *our* educations commonly like a pile of books laid over a plant in a pot? The compressed nature struggles through at every crevice, but can never get the cramp and stunt out of it. We spend all our youth in building a vessel for our voyage of life, and set forth with streamers flying; but the moment we come nigh the great loadstone mountain of our proper destiny, out leap all our carefully-driven bolts and nails, and we get many a mouthful of good salt brine, and many a buffet of the rough water of experience, before we secure the bare right to live.

We now entered the outlet, a long-drawn aisle of alder, on each side of which spired tall firs, spruces, and white cedars. The motion of the birch reminded me of the gondola, and they represent among water-craft the *felidæ*, the cat tribe, stealthy, silent, treacherous, and preying by night. I closed my eyes, and strove to fancy myself in the dumb city, whose only horses are the bronze ones of St. Mark. But Nature would allow no rival, and bent down an alder-bough to brush my cheek and recall me. Only the robin sings in the emerald chambers of these tall sylvan palaces, and the squirrel leaps from hanging balcony to balcony.

The rain which the loons foreboded had raised the west branch of the Penobscot so much, that a strong current was setting back into the pond; and, when at last we brushed through into the river, it was full to the brim, — too full for moose, the hunters said. Rivers with low banks have always the compensation of giving a sense of entire fulness. The sun sank behind its horizon of pines, whose pointed summits notched the rosy west in an endless black *sierra*. At the same moment the golden moon swung slowly up in the east, like the other scale of that Homeric balance in which Zeus weighed the deeds of men. Sunset and moonrise at once! Adam had no more in Eden — except the head of Eve upon his shoulder. The stream was so smooth, that the floating logs we met seemed to hang in a glowing atmosphere, the shadow-half being as real as the solid. And gradually the mind was etherized to a like dreamy placidity, till fact and fancy, the substance and the image, floating on the current of reverie, became but as the upper and under halves of one unreal reality.

In the west still lingered a pale-green light. I do not know whether it be from greater familiarity, but it always seems to me that the pinnacles of pine-trees make an edge to the landscape which tells better against the twilight, or the fainter dawn before the rising moon, than the rounded and cloud-cumulus outline of hard-wood trees.

After paddling a couple of miles, we found the arbored mouth of the little Malahoodus River, famous for moose. We had been on the look-out for it, and I was amused to hear one of the hunters say to the other, to assure himself of his familiarity with the spot, "You *drove* the West Branch last spring, did n't you?" as one of us might ask about a horse. We did not explore the Malahoodus far, but left the other birch to thread its cedared solitudes, while we turned back to try our fortunes in the larger stream. We paddled on about four miles farther, lingering now and then opposite the black mouth of a moose-path. The incidents of our voyage were few, but quite as exciting and profitable as the *items* of the newspapers. A stray log compensated very well for the ordinary run of accidents, and the floating *carkiss* of a moose which we met could pass muster instead of a singular discovery of human remains by workmen in digging a cellar. Once or twice we saw what seemed ghosts of trees; but they turned out to be dead cedars, in winding-sheets of long gray moss, made spectral by the moonlight. Just as we were turning to drift back down-stream, we heard a loud gnawing sound close by us on the bank. One of our guides thought it a hedgehog, the other a bear. I inclined to the bear, as making the adventure more imposing. A rifle was fired at the sound, which began again with the most provoking indifference, ere the echo, flaring madly at first from shore to shore, died far away in a hoarse sigh.

Half past Eleven, P. M. — No sign of a

moose yet. The birch, it seems, was strained at the Carry, or the pitch was softened as she lay on the shore during dinner, and she leaks a little. If there be any virtue in the *sitzbad*, I shall discover it. If I cannot extract green cucumbers from the moon's rays, I get something quite as cool. One of the guides shivers so as to shake the birch.

Quarter to Twelve. — *Later from the Freshet!* — The water in the birch is about three inches deep, but the dampness reaches already nearly to the waist. I am obliged to remove the matches from the ground-floor of my trousers into the upper story of a breast-pocket. Meanwhile, we are to sit immovable, — for fear of frightening the moose, — which induces cramps.

Half past Twelve. — A crashing is heard on the left bank. This is a moose in good earnest. We are besought to hold our breaths, if possible. My fingers so numb, I could not, if I tried. *Crash! crash!* again, and then a plunge, followed by dead stillness. " Swimmin' crik," whispers guide, suppressing all unnecessary parts of speech, — "don't stir." I, for one, am not likely to. A cold fog which has been gathering for the last hour has finished me. I fancy myself one of those naked pigs that seem rushing out of market-doors in winter, frozen in a ghastly attitude of gallop. If I were to be shot myself, I should feel no interest in it. As it is, I am only a spectator, having declined a gun. *Splash!* again; this time the moose is in sight, and *click! click!* one rifle misses fire after the other. The fog has quietly spiked our batteries. The moose goes crashing up the bank, and presently we can hear it chewing its cud close by. So we lie in wait, freezing.

At one o'clock, I propose to land at a deserted *wongen* I had noticed on the way up, where I will make a fire, and leave them to refrigerate as much longer as they please. Axe in hand, I go plunging through waist-deep weeds dripping with dew, haunted by an intense conviction that the gnawing sound we had heard *was* a bear, and a bear at least eighteen hands high. There is something pokerish about a deserted dwelling, even in broad daylight; but here in the obscure wood, and the moon filtering unwillingly through the trees! Well, I made the door at last, and found the place packed fuller with darkness than it ever had been with hay. Gradually I was able to make things out a little, and began to hack frozenly at a log which I groped out. I was relieved presently by one of the guides. He cut at once into one of the uprights of the building till he got some dry splinters, and we soon had a fire like the burning of a whole wood-wharf in our part of the country. My companion went back to the birch, and left me to keep house. First I knocked a hole in the roof (which the fire began to lick in a relishing way) for a chimney, and then cleared away a damp growth of " pison-elder," to make a sleeping place. When the unsuccessful hunters returned, I had everything quite comfortable, and was steaming at the rate of about ten horse-power a minute. Young Telemachus was sorry to give up the moose so soon, and, with the teeth chattering almost out of his head, he declared that he would like to stick it out all night. However, he reconciled himself to the fire, and, making our beds of some "splits" which we poked from the roof, we lay down at half past two. I, who have inherited a habit of looking into every closet before I go to bed, for fear of fire, had become in two days such a stoic of the woods, that I went to sleep tranquilly, certain that my bedroom would be in a blaze before morning. And so, indeed, it was; and the withes that bound it together being burned off, one of the sides fell in without waking me.

Tuesday, 16*th*. — After a sleep of two hours and a half, so sound that it was as good as tight, we started at half past four for the haymakers' camp again. We found them just getting breakfast. We sat down upon the *deacon-seat* before the fire blazing between the bedroom and the *salle à manger*, which were simply two roofs of spruce-bark, sloping to the ground on one side, the other three being left open. We found that we had, at least, been luckier than the other party, for M. had brought back his convoy without even seeing a moose. As there was not room at the table for all of us to breakfast together, these hospitable woodmen forced us to sit down first, although we resisted stoutly. Our breakfast consisted of fresh bread, fried salt pork, stewed whortleberries, and tea. Our kind hosts refused to take money for it, nor would M. accept anything for his trouble. This seemed even more open-handed when I remembered that they had brought all their stores over the Carry upon their shoulders, paying an ache *extra* for every pound. If their hospitality lacked anything of hard external polish, it had all the deeper grace which springs only from sincere manliness. I have rarely sat at a *table d'hôte* wh'ch might not have taken a lesson from them in essential courtesy. I have never seen a finer race of men. They have all the virtues of the sailor, without that unsteady roll in the gait with which the ocean proclaims itself quite as much in the moral as in the physical habit of a man. They appeared to me to have hewn out a short northwest passage through wintry woods to those spice-lands of character which we dwellers in cities must reach, if at all, by weary voyages in the monotonous track of the trades.

By the way, as we were embirching last evening for our moose-chase, I asked what I was to do with my baggage. "Leave it here," said our guide, and he laid the bags upon a platform of alders, which he bent down to keep them beyond reach of the rising water.

"Will they be safe here?"

"As safe as they would be locked up in your house at home."

And so I found them at my return; only the hay-makers had carried them to their camp for greater security against the chances of the weather.

We got back to Kineo in time for dinner; and in the afternoon, the weather being fine, went up the mountain. As we landed at the foot, our guide pointed to the remains of a red shirt and a pair of blanket trousers. "That," said he, " is the reason there 's such a trade in ready-made clo'es. A suit gits pooty well wore out by the time a camp breaks up in the spring, and the lumberers want to look about right when they come back into the settlements, so they buy somethin' ready-made, and heave ole bust-up into the bush." True enough, thought I, this is the Ready-made Age. It is quicker being covered than fitted. So we all go to the slop-shop and come out uniformed, every mother's son with habits of thinking and doing cut on one pattern, with no special reference to his peculiar build.

Kineo rises 1750 feet above the sea, and 150 above the lake. The climb is very easy, with fine outlooks at every turn over lake and forest. Near the top is a spring of water, which even Uncle Zeb might have allowed to be wholesome. The little tin dipper was scratched all over with names, showing that vanity, at least, is not put out of breath by the ascent. O Ozymandias, King of kings! We are all scrawling on something of the kind. "My name is engraved on the institutions of my country," thinks the statesman. But, alas! institutions are as changeable as tin-dippers; men are content to drink the same old water, if the shape of the cup only be new, and our friend gets two lines in the Biographical Dictionaries. After all, these inscriptions, which make us smile up here, are about as valuable as the Assyrian ones which Hincks and Rawlinson read at cross-purposes. Have we not Smiths and Browns enough, that we must ransack the ruins of Nimroud for more? Near the spring we met a Bloomer! It was the first chronic one I had ever seen. It struck me as a sensible costume for the occasion, and it will be the only wear in the Greek Kalends, when women believe that sense is an equivalent for grace.

The forest primeval is best seen from the top of a mountain. It then impresses one by its extent, like an Oriental epic. To be in it is nothing, for then an acre is as good as a thousand square miles. You cannot see five rods in any direction, and the ferns, mosses, and tree-trunks just around you are the best of it. As for solitude, night will make a better one with ten feet square of pitch dark; and mere size is hardly an element of grandeur, except in works of man,— as the Colosseum. It is through one or the other pole of vanity that men feel the sublime in mountains. It is either, How small great I am beside it! or, Big as you are, little I's soul will hold a dozen of you. The true idea of a forest is not a *selva selvaggia*, but something humanized a little, as we imagine the forest of Arden, with trees standing at royal intervals, — a commonwealth, and not a communism. To some moods, it is congenial to ook over endless leagues of unbroken sav gery without a hint of man.

Wednesday. — This morning fished. Telemachus caught a *laker* of thirteen pounds and a half, and I an overgrown cusk, which we threw away, but which I found afterwards Agassiz would have been glad of, for all is fish that comes to his net, from the fossil down. The fish, when caught, are straightway knocked on the head. A lad who went with us seeming to show an over-zeal in this operation, we remonstrated. But he gave a good, human reason for it, — "He no need to ha' gone and been a fish if he did n't like it," — an excuse which superior strength or cunning has always found sufficient. It was some comfort, in this case, to think that St. Jerome believed in a limitation of God's providence, and that it did not extend to inanimate things or creatures devoid of reason.

Thus, my dear Storg, I have finished my Oriental adventures, and somewhat, it must be owned, in the diffuse Oriental manner. There is very little about Moosehead Lake in it, and not even the Latin name for moose, which I might have obtained by sufficient research. If I had killed one, I would have given you his name in that dead language. I did not profess to give you an account of the lake; but a journal, and, moreover, *my* journal, with a little nature, a little human nature, and a great deal of I in it, which last ingredient I take to be the true spirit of this species of writing; all the rest being so much water for tender throats which **cannot take it neat.**

Leaves

from

My Journal in Italy

and elsewhere.

AT SEA.

THE sea was meant to be looked at from shore, as mountains are from the plain. Lucretius made this discovery long ago, and was blunt enough to blurt it forth, romance and sentiment — in other words, the pretence of feeling what we do not feel — being inventions of a later day. To be sure, Cicero used to twaddle about Greek literature and philosophy, much as people do about ancient art now-a-days; but I rather sympathize with those stout old Romans who despised both, and believed that to found an empire was as grand an achievement as to build an epic or to carve a statue. But though there might have been twaddle, (as why not, since there was a Senate?) I rather think Petrarch was the first choragus of that sentimental dance which so long led young folks away from the realities of life like the piper of Hamelin, and whose succession ended, let us hope, with Chateaubriand. But for them, Byron, whose real strength lay in his sincerity, would never have talked about the " sea bounding beneath him like a steed that knows his rider," and all that sort of thing. Even if it had been true, steam has been as fatal to that part of the romance of the sea as to hand-loom weaving. But what say you to a twelve days' calm such as we dozed through in mid-Atlantic and in mid-August? I know nothing so tedious at once and exasperating as that regular slap of the wilted sails when the ship rises and falls with the slow breathing of the sleeping sea, one greasy, brassy swell following another, slow, smooth, immitigable as the series of Wordsworth's " Ecclesiastical Sonnets." Even at his best, Neptune, in a *tête-à-tête*, has a way of repeating himself, an obtuseness to the *ne quid nimis*, that is stupefying. It reminds me of organ-music and my good friend Sebastian

Bach. A fugue or two will do very well; but a concert made up of nothing else is altogether too epic for me. There is nothing so desperately monotonous as the sea, and I no longer wonder at the cruelty of pirates. Fancy an existence in which the coming up of a clumsy finback whale, who says *Pooh!* to you solemnly as you lean over the taffrail, is an event as exciting as an election on shore! The dampness seems to strike into the wits as into the lucifer-matches, so that one may scratch a thought half a dozen times and get nothing at last but a faint sputter, the forlorn hope of fire, which only goes far enough to leave a sense of suffocation behind it. Even smoking becomes an employment instead of a solace. Who less likely to come to their wit's end than W. M. T. and A. H. C.? Yet I have seen them driven to five meals a day for mental occupation. I sometimes sit and pity Noah; but even he had this advantage over all succeeding navigators, that, wherever he landed, he was sure to get no ill news from home. He should be canonized as the patron-saint of newspaper correspondents, being the only man who ever had the very last authentic intelligence from everywhere.

The finback whale recorded just above has much the look of a brown-paper parcel, — the whitish stripes that run across him answering for the pack-thread. He has a kind of accidental hole in the top of his head, through which he *pooh-poohs* the rest of creation, and which looks as if it had been made by the chance thrust of a chestnut rail. He was our first event. Our second was harpooning a sunfish, which basked dozing on the lap of the sea, looking so much like the giant turtle of an alderman's dream, that I am persuaded he would have made mock-turtle soup rather than acknowledge his imposture. But he broke away just as they were hauling him over the side, and sank placidly through the clear water, leaving behind him a crimson trail that wavered a moment and was gone.

The sea, though, has better sights than these.

When we were up with the Azores, we began to meet flying-fish and Portuguese men-of-war beautiful as the galley of Cleopatra, tiny craft that dared these seas before Columbus. I have seen one of the former rise from the crest of a wave, and, glancing from another some two hundred feet beyond, take a fresh flight of perhaps as long. How Calderon would have similized this pretty creature had he ever seen it! How would he have run him up and down the gamut of simile! If a fish, then a fish with wings; if a bird, then a bird with fins; and so on, keeping up the poor shuttle-cock of a conceit as is his wont. Indeed, the poor thing is the most killing bait for a comparison, and I assure you I have three or four in my inkstand;—but be calm, they shall stay there. Moore, who looked on all nature as a kind of *Gradus ad Parnassum*, a *thesaurus* of similitude, and spent his life in a game of What is my thought like? with himself, *did* the flying-fish on his way to Bermuda. So I leave him in peace.

The most beautiful thing I have seen at sea, all the more so that I had never heard of it, is the trail of a shoal of fish through the phosphorescent water. It is like a flight of silver rockets, or the streaming of northern lights through that silent nether heaven. I thought nothing could go beyond that rustling starfoam which was churned up by our ship's bows, or those eddies and disks of dreamy flame that rose and wandered out of sight behind us.

> 'T was fire our ship was plunging through,
> Cold fire that o'er the quarter flew;
> And wandering moons of idle flame
> Grew full and waned, and went and came,
> Dappling with light the huge sea-snake
> That slid behind us in the wake.

But there was something even more delicately rare in the apparition of the fish, as they turned up in gleaming furrows the latent moonshine which the ocean seemed to have hoarded against these vacant interlunar nights. In the Mediterranean one day, as we were lying becalmed, I observed the water freckled with dingy specks, which at last gathered to a pinkish scum on the surface. The sea had been so phosphorescent for some nights, that when the Captain gave me my bath, by dousing me with buckets from the house on deck, the spray flew off my head and shoulders in sparks. It occurred to me that this dirty-looking scum might be the luminous matter, and I had a pailful dipped up to keep till after dark. When I went to look at it after nightfall, it seemed at first perfectly dead; but when I shook it, the whole broke out into what I can only liken to milky flames, whose lambent silence was strangely beautiful, and startled me almost as actual projection might an alchemist. I could not bear to be the death of so much beauty; so I poured it all overboard again.

Another sight worth taking a voyage for is that of the sails by moonlight. Our course was "south and by east, half south," so that we seemed bound for the full moon as she rolled up over our wavering horizon. Then I used to go forward to the bowsprit and look back. Our ship was a clipper, with every rag set, stunsails, sky-scrapers, and all; nor was it easy to believe that such a wonder could be built of canvas as that white many-storied pile of cloud that stooped over me, or drew back as we rose and fell with the waves.

These are all the wonders I can recall of my five weeks at sea, except the sun. Were you ever alone with the sun? You think it a very simple question; but I never was, in the full sense of the word, till I was held up to him one cloudless day on the broad buckler of the ocean. I suppose one might have the same feeling in the desert. I remember getting something like it years ago, when I climbed alone to the top of a mountain, and lay face up on the hot gray moss, striving to get a notion of how an Arab might feel. It was my American commentary of the Koran, and not a bad one. In a New England winter, too, when everything is gagged with snow as if some gigantic physical geographer were taking a cast of the earth's face in plaster, the bare knob of a hill will introduce you to the sun as a comparative stranger. But at sea you may be alone with him day after day, and almost all day long. I never understood before that nothing short of full daylight can give the supremest sense of solitude. Darkness will not do so, for the imagination peoples it with more shapes than ever were poured from the frozen loins of the populous North. The sun, I sometimes think, is a little *grouty* at sea, especially at high noon, feeling that he wastes his beams on those fruitless furrows. It is otherwise with the moon. She "comforts the night," as Chapman finely says, and I always found her a companionable creature.

In the ocean-horizon I took untiring delight. It is the true magic-circle of expectation and conjecture, — almost as good as a wishing-ring. What will rise over that edge we sail toward daily and never overtake? A sail? an island? the new shore of the Old World?

Something rose every day, which I need not have gone so far to see, but at whose levee I was a much more faithful courtier than on shore. A cloudless sunrise in mid-ocean is beyond comparison for simple grandeur. It is like Dante's style, bare and perfect. Naked sun meets naked sea, the true classic of nature. There may be more sentiment in morning on shore, — the shivering fairy-jewelry of dew, the silver point-lace of sparkling hoar-frost, — but there is also more complexity, more of the romantic. The one savors of the elder Edda, the other of the Minnesingers.

> And I thus floating, lonely elf,
> A kind of planet by myself,
> The mists draw up and furl away,
> And in the east a warming gray,
> Faint as the tint of oaken woods
> When o'er their buds May breathes and broods,
> Tells that the golden sunrise-tide
> Is lapsing up earth's thirsty side,
> Each moment purpling on the crest
> Of some stark billow farther west:
> And as the sea-moss droops and hears
> The gurgling flood that nears and nears,

And then with tremulous content
Floats out each thankful filament,
So waited I until it came,
God's daily miracle, — O shame
That I had seen so many days
Unthankful, without wondering praise,
Not recking more this bliss of earth
Than the cheap fire that lights my hearth!
But now glad thoughts and holy pour
Into my heart, as once a year
To San Miniato's open door,
In long procession, chanting clear,
Through slopes of sun, through shadows hoar,
The coupled monks slow-climbing sing,
And like a golden censer swing
From rear to front, from front to rear
Their alternating bursts of praise,
Till the roof's fading seraphs gaze
Down through an odorous mist, that crawls
Lingeringly up the darkened walls,
And the dim arches, silent long,
Are startled with triumphant song.

I wrote yesterday that the sea still rimmed our prosy lives with mystery and conjecture. But one is shut up on shipboard like Montaigne in his tower, with nothing to do but to review his own thoughts and contradict himself. *Dire, redire, et me contredire,* will be the staple of my journal till I see land. I say nothing of such matters as the *montagna bruna* on which Ulysses wrecked; but since the sixteenth century could any man reasonably hope to stumble on one of those wonders which were cheap as dirt in the days of St. Saga? Faustus, Don Juan, and Tanhaüser are the last ghosts of legend, that lingered almost till the Gallic cock-crow of universal enlightenment and disillusion. The Public School has done for Imagination. What shall I see in Outre-Mer, or on the way thither, but what can be seen with eyes? To be sure, I stick by the sea-serpent, and would fain believe that science has scotched, not killed, him. Nor is he to be lightly given up, for, like the old Scandinavian snake, he binds together for us the two hemispheres of Past and Present, of Belief and Science. He is the link which knits us seaboard Yankees with our Norse progenitors, interpreting between the age of the dragon and that of the railroad-train

We have made ducks and drakes of that large estate of wonder and delight bequeathed to us by ancestral vikings, and this alone remains to us unthrift heirs of Linn.

I feel an undefined respect for a man who has seen the sea-serpent. He is to his brother-fishers what the poet is to his fellow-men. Where they have seen nothing better than a school of horse-mackerel, or the idle coils of ocean around Half-way Rock, he has caught authentic glimpses of the withdrawing mantle-hem of the Edda age. I care not for the monster himself. It is not the thing, but the belief in the thing, that is dear to me. May it be long before Professor Owen is comforted with the sight of his unfleshed vertebræ, long before they stretch many a rood behind Kimball's or Barnum's glass, reflected in the shallow orbs of Mr. and Mrs. Public, which stare, but see not! When we read that Captain Spalding, of the pink-stern *Three Pollies*, has beheld him rushing through the brine like an infinite series of bewitched mackerel-casks, we feel that the mystery of old Ocean, at least, has not yet been sounded, — that Faith and Awe survive there unevaporate. I once ventured the horse-mackerel theory to an old fisherman, browner than a tomcod. "Hos-mackril!" he exclaimed indignantly, "hos-mackril be — " (here he used a phrase commonly indicated in laical literature by the same sign which serves for Doctorate in Divinity,) "don't yer spose *I* know a hos-mackril?" The intonation of that "*I*" would have silenced Professor Monkbarns Owen with his provoking *phoca* forever. What if one should ask *him* if he knew a trilobite?

The fault of modern travellers is, that they see nothing out of sight. They talk of eocene periods and tertiary formations, and tell us how the world looked to the plesiosaur. They take science (or nescience) with them, instead of that soul of generous trust their elders had. All their senses are sceptics and doubters, materialists reporting things for other sceptics to doubt still further upon. Nature be comes a reluctant witness upon the stand, badgered with geologist hammers and phials of acid. There have been no travellers since those included in Hakluyt and Purchas, except Martin, perhaps, who saw an inch or two into the invisible at the Orkneys. We have peripatetic lecturers, but no more travellers. Travellers' stories are no longer proverbial. We have picked nearly every apple (wormy or otherwise) from the world's tree of knowledge, and that without an Eve to tempt us. Two or three have hitherto hung luckily beyond reach on a lofty bough shadowing the interior of Africa, but there is a German Doctor at this very moment pelting at them with sticks and stones. It may be only next week, and these too, bitten by geographers and geologists, will be thrown away.

Analysis is carried into everything. Even Deity is subjected to chemic tests. We must have exact knowledge, a cabinet stuck full of facts pressed, dried, or preserved in spirits, instead of the large, vague world our fathers had. With them science was poetry; with us, poetry is science. Our modern Eden is a *hortus siccus*. Tourists defraud rather than enrich us. They have not that sense of æsthetic proportion which characterized the elder traveller. Earth is no longer the fine work of art it was, for nothing is left to the imagination. Job Hortop, arrived at the height of the Bermudas, thinks it full time to indulge us in a merman. Nay, there is a story told by Webster, in his "Witchcraft," of a merman with a mitre, who, on being sent back to his watery diocese of finland, made what advances he could toward an episcopal benediction by bowing his head thrice. Doubtless he had been consecrated by St. Antony of Padua. A dumb bishop would be sometimes no unpleasant phenomenon, by the way. Sir John Hawkins is not satisfied with telling us about the merely sensual Canaries, but is generous enough to throw us in a handful of "certain flitting islands" to boot. Henry Hawkes describes the visible Mexican cities and then is not so frugal but that he can give us a few invisible ones. Thus do these generous ancient mariners make children of us again. Their successors show us an earth effete and past bearing, tracing out with the eyes of industrious fleas every wrinkle and crowfoot.

The journals of the elder navigators are prose Odysseys. The geographies of our ancestors were works of fancy and imagination. They read poems where we yawn over items. Their world was a huge wonder-horn, exhaustless as that which Thor strove to drain. Ours would scarce quench the small thirst of a bee. No modern voyager brings back the magical foundation-stones of a Tempest. No Marco Polo, traversing the desert beyond the city of Lok, would tell of things able to inspire the mind of Milton with

> "Calling shapes and beckoning shadows dire,
> And airy tongues that syllable men's names
> On sands and shores and desert wildernesses."

It was easy enough to believe the story of

Dante, when two thirds of even the upper-world were yet untraversed and unmapped. With every step of the recent traveller our inheritance of the wonderful is diminished. Those beautifully pictured notes of the Possible are redeemed at a ruinous discount in the hard and cumbrous coin of the Actual. How are we not defrauded and impoverished? Does California vie with El Dorado? or are Bruce's Abyssinian kings a set-off for Prester John? A bird in the bush is worth two in the hand. And if the philosophers have not even yet been able to agree whether the world has any existence independent of ourselves, how do we not gain a loss in every addition to the catalogue of Vulgar Errors? Where are the fishes which nidificated in trees? Where the monopodes sheltering themselves from the sun beneath their single umbrella-like foot, — umbrella-like in everything but the fatal necessity of being borrowed? Where the Acephali, with whom Herodotus, in a kind of ecstasy wound up his climax of men with abnormal top-pieces ? Where the Roc whose eggs are possibly boulders, needing no far-fetched theory of glacier or iceberg to account for them? Where the tails of the men of Kent? Where the no legs of the bird of paradise? Where the Unicorn, with that single horn of his, sovereign against all manner of poisons? Where the Fountain of Youth? Where that Thessalian spring, which, without cost to the country, convicted and punished perjurers? Where the Amazons of Orellana? All these, and a thousand other varieties, we have lost, and have got nothing instead of them. And those who have robbed us of them have stolen that which not enriches themselves. It is so much wealth cast into the sea beyond all approach of diving-bells. We owe no thanks to Mr. J. E. Worcester, whose Geography we studied enforcedly at school. Yet even he had his relentings, and in some softer moment vouchsafed us a fine, inspiring print of the Maelstrom, answerable to the twenty-four mile diameter of its suction. Year by year, more and more of the world gets disenchanted. Even the icy privacy of the arctic and antarctic circles is invaded. Our youth are no longer ingenious, as indeed no ingenuity is demanded of them. Everything is accounted for, everything cut and dried, and the world may be put together as easily as the fragments of a dissected map. The Mysterious bounds nothing now on the North, South, East, or West. We have played Jack Horner with our earth, till there is never a plum left in it.

IN THE MEDITERRANEAN.

THE first sight of a shore so historical as that of Europe gives an American a strange thrill. What we always feel the artistic want of at home, is background. It is all idle to say we are Englishmen, and that English history is ours too. It is precisely in this that we are *not* Englishmen, inasmuch as we only possess their history through our minds, and not by life-long association with a spot and an idea we call England. History without the soil it grew in, is more instructive than inspiring, — an acquisition, and not an inheritance. It is laid away in our memories, and does not run in our veins. Surely, in all that concerns æsthetics, Europeans have us at an immense advantage. They start at a point which we arrive at after weary years, for literature is not shut up in books, nor art in galleries:

both are taken in by unconscious absorption through the finer pores of mind and character in the atmosphere of society. We are not yet out of our Crusoe-hood, and must make our own tools as best we may. Yet I think we shall find the good of it one of these days, in being thrown back more wholly on nature; and our literature, when we have learned to feel our own strength, and to respect our own thought because it is ours, and not because the European Mrs. Grundy agrees with it, will have a fresh flavor and a strong body that will recommend it, especially as what we import is watered more and more liberally with every vintage.

My first glimpse of Europe was the shore of Spain. Since we got into the Mediterranean, we have been becalmed for some days within easy view of it. All along are fine mountains, brown all day, and with a bloom on them at sunset like that of a ripe plum Here and there at their feet little white towns are sprinkled along the edge of the water, like the grains of rice dropped by the princess in the story. Sometimes we see larger buildings on the mountain slopes, probably convents. I sit and wonder whether the farther peaks may not be the Sierra Morena (the rusty saw) of Don Quixote. I resolve that they shall be, and am content. Surely latitude and longitude never showed me any particular respect, that I should be over-scrupulous with them.

But after all, Nature, though she may be more beautiful, is nowhere so entertaining as in man, and the best thing I have seen and learned at sea is our Chief Mate. My first acquaintance with him was made over my knife, which he asked to look at, and, after a critical examination, handed back to me, saying, "I should n't wonder if that 'ere was a good piece o' stuff." Since then he has transferred a part of his regard for my knife to its owner. I like folks who like an honest bit of steel, and take no interest whatever in "your Raphaels, Correggios, and stuff." There is always more than the average human nature in a man who has a hearty sympathy with iron. It is a manly metal, with no sordid associations like gold and silver. My sailor fully came up to my expectation on further acquaintance. He might well be called an old salt who had been wrecked on Spitzbergen before I was born. He was not an American, but I should never have guessed it by his speech, which was the purest Cape Cod, and I reckon myself a good taster of dialects. Nor was he less Americanized in all his thoughts and feelings, a singular proof of the ease with which our omnivorous country assimilates foreign matter, provided it be Protestant, for he was a man ere he became an American citizen. He used to walk the deck with his hands in his pockets, in seeming abstraction, but nothing escaped his eye. *How* he saw, I could never make out, though I had a theory that it was with his elbows. After he had taken me (or my knife) into his confidence, he took care that I should see whatever he deemed of interest to a landsman. Without looking up, he would say, suddenly, "Ther's a whale blowin' clearn up to win'ard," or, "Them's porpises to leeward: that means chănge o' wind." He is as impervious to cold as a polar bear, and paces the deck during his watch much as one of those yellow hummocks goes slumping up and down his cage. On the Atlantic, if the wind blew a gale from the northeast, and it was cold as an English summer, he was sure to turn out in a calico shirt and trousers, his furzy brown chest half bare, and slippers, without stockings. But lest you might fancy this to have chanced by defect of wardrobe, he comes out in a monstrous pea-jacket here in the Mediterranean, when the evening is so hot that Adam would have been glad to leave off his fig-leaves. "It's a kind o' damp and unwholesome in these ere waters," he says, evidently regarding the Midland Sea as a vile standing pool, in comparison with the bluff ocean. At meals he is superb, not only for his strengths, but his weaknesses. He has some how or other come to think me a wag, and if I ask him to pass the butter, detects an occult joke, and laughs as much as is proper for a mate. For you must know that our social hierarchy on shipboard is precise, and the second mate, were he present, would only laugh half as much as the first. Mr. X. always combs his hair, and works himself into a black frock-coat (on Sundays he adds a waistcoat) before he comes to meals, sacrificing himself nobly and painfully to the social proprieties. The second mate, on the other hand, who eats after us, enjoys the privilege of shirt-sleeves, and is, I think, the happier man of the two. We do not have seats above and below the salt, as in old time, but above and below the white sugar. Mr. X. always takes brown sugar, and it is delightful to see how he ignores the existence of certain delicates which he considers above his grade, tipping his head on one side with an air of abstraction, so that he may seem not to deny himself, but to omit helping himself from inadvertence or absence of mind. At such times he wrinkles his forehead in a peculiar manner, inscrutable at first as a cuneiform inscription, but as easily read after you once get the key. The sense of it is something like this: " I, X., know my place, a height of wisdom attained by few. Whatever you may think, I do *not* see that currant jelly, nor that preserved grape. Especially, a kind Providence has made me blind to bowls of white sugar, and deaf to the pop of champagne corks. It is much that a merciful compensation gives me a sense of the dingier hue of Havana, and the muddier gurgle of beer. Are there potted meats? My physician has ordered me three pounds of minced salt-junk at every meal." There is such a thing, you know, as a ship's husband: X. is the ship's poor relation.

As I have said, he takes also a below-the-white-sugar interest in the jokes, laughing by precise point of compass, just as he would lay the ship's course, all *yawing* being out of the question with his scrupulous decorum at the helm. Once or twice I have got the better of him, and touched him off into a kind of compromised explosion, like that of damp fireworks, that splutter and simmer a little, and then go out with painful slowness and occasional relapses. But his fuse is always of the unwillingest, and you must blow your match, and touch him off again and again with the same joke. Or rather, you must magnetize him many times to get him *en rapport* with a jest. This once accomplished, you have him, and one bit of fun will last the whole voyage. He prefers those of one syllable, the *a-b abs* of humor. The gradual fattening of the steward, a benevolent mulatto with whiskers and ear-rings, who looks as if he had been meant for a woman, and had become a man by accident, as in some of those stories of the elder physiologists, is an abiding topic of humorous comment with Mr X. "That 'ere stooard," he says, with a brown grin like what you might fancy on the face of a serious and aged seal, " 's agittin' as fat 's a porpis. He was as thin 's a shingle when he come aboord last v'yge. Them trousis 'll bust yit. He don't darst take 'em off nights, for the whole ship's company could n't git him into 'em agin." And then he turns aside to enjoy the intensity of his emotion by himself, and you hear at intervals low rumblings, an indigestion of laughter. He tells me of St. Elmo's fires, Marvell's *corposants*, though with him the original *corpos santos* has suffered a sea change, and turned to *comepleasants*, pledges of fine weather. I shall not soon find a pleasanter companion. It is so delightful to meet a man who knows just what you do *not*. Nay, I think the tired mind finds something in plump ignorance like what the body feels in cushiony moss. Talk of the sympathy of kindred pursuits! It is the sympathy of the upper and nether millstones, both forever grinding the same grist, and wearing each other smooth.

One has not far to seek for book-nature, artist-nature, every variety of superinduced nature, in short, but genuine human-nature is hard to find. And how good it is! Wholesome as a potato, fit company for any dish. The freemasonry of cultivated men is agreeable, but artificial, and I like better the natural grip with which manhood recognizes manhood.

X. has one good story, and with that I leave him, wishing him with all my heart that little inland farm at last which is his calenture as he paces the windy deck. One evening, when the clouds looked wild and whirling, I asked X. if it was coming on to blow. "No, I guess not," said he; "bumby the moon 'll be up, and scoff away that 'ere loose stuff." His intonation set the phrase "scoff away" in quotation-marks as plain as print. So I put a query in each eye, and he went on. "Ther' was a Dutch cappen onct, an his mate come to him in the cabin, where he sot takin˚ his schnapps, an' says, 'Cappen, it's agittin' thick, an' looks kin' o' squally hed n't we 's good 's shorten sail?' 'Gimmy my alminick,' says the cappen. So he looks at it a spell, an' says he, 'The moon 's due in less 'n half an hour, an' she 'll scoff away ev'ythin' clare agin.' So the mate he goes, an' bumby down he comes agin, an' says, 'Cappen, this 'ere 's the allfiredest, powerfullest moon 't ever you *did* see. She 's scoffed away the maintogallants'l, an' she 's to work on the foretops'l now. Guess you 'd better look in the alminick agin, an' fin' out when *this* moon sets.' So the cappen thought 't was 'bout time to go on deck. Dreadful slow them Dutch cappens be." And X. walked away, rumbling inwardly, like the rote of the sea heard afar.

And so we arrived at Malta. Did you ever hear of one of those eating-houses, where, for a certain fee, the guest has the right to make one thrust with a fork into a huge pot, in which the whole dinner is bubbling, getting perhaps a bit of boiled meat, or a potato, or else nothing? Well, when the great caldron of war is seething, and the nations stand round it striving to fish out something to their purpose from the mess, Britannia always has a great advantage in her trident. Malta is one of the titbits she has impaled with that awful implement. I was not sorry for it, when I reached my clean inn, with its kindly English landlady.

ITALY.

THE impulse which sent the Edelmann Storg and me to Subiaco was given something like two thousand years ago. Had we not seen the Ponte Sant' Antonio, we should not have gone to Subiaco at this particular time ; and had the Romans been worse masons, or more ignorant of hydrodynamics than they were, we should never have seen the Ponte Sant' Antonio. But first we went to Tivoli, — two carriage-loads of us, a very agreeable mixture of English, Scotch, and Yankees, — on Tuesday, the 20th April. I shall not say anything about Tivoli. A water-fall in type is likely to be a trifle stiffish. Old association and modern beauty ; nature and artifice ; worship that has passed away and the religion that abides forever ·

the green gush of the deeper torrent and the white evanescence of innumerable cascades, delicately palpitant as a fall of northern lights; the descendants of Sabine pigeons flashing up to immemorial dove-cots, for centuries inaccessible to man, trooping with noisy rooks and daws; the fitful roar and the silently hovering iris, which, borne by the wind across the face of the cliff, transmutes the travertine to momentary opal, and whose dimmer ghost haunts the moonlight, — as well attempt to describe to a Papuan savage that wondrous ode of Wordsworth which rouses and stirs in the soul all its dormant instincts of resurrection as with a sound of the last trumpet. No, it is impossible. Even Byron's pump *sucks* sometimes, and gives an unpleasant dry wheeze, especially, it seems to me, at Terni. It is guide-book poetry, enthusiasm manufactured by the yard, which the hurried traveller (John and Jonathan are always in a hurry when they turn peripatetics) puts on when ne has not a rag of private imagination to cover his nakedness withal. It must be a queer kind of love that could " watch madness with unalterable mien," when the patient, whom any competent physician would have ordered into a strait-waistcoat long ago, has shivered himself to powder down a precipice. But there is no madness in the matter. Velino goes over in his full senses, and knows perfectly well that he shall not be hurt, that his broken fragments will reunite more glibly than the head and neck of Orrilo. He leaps exultant, as to his proper doom and fulfilment, and out of the mere waste and spray of his glory the god of sunshine and song builds over the crowning moment of his destiny a triumphal arch beyond the reach of time and of decay. But Milton is the only man who has got much poetry out of a cataract, — and that was a cataract in his eye.

The first day we made the *Giro*, coming back to a merry dinner at the Sibilla in the evening. Then we had some special tea, — for the Italians think tea-drinking the chief religious observance of the *Inglesi,* — and then we had fifteen pauls' worth of illumination, which wrought a sudden change in the scenery, like those that seem so matter-of-course in dreams, turning the Claude we had seen in the morning into a kind of Piranesi-Rembrandt. The illumination, by the way, which had been prefigured to us by the enthusiastic Italian who conducted it as something second only to the *Girandola,* turned out to be one blue-light and two armfuls of straw.

The Edelmann Storg is not fond of pedestrian locomotion, — nay, I have even sometimes thought that he looked upon the invention of legs as a private and personal wrong done to himself. I am quite sure that he inwardly believes them to have been a consequence of the fall, and that the happier Pre-Adamites were monopodes, and incapable of any but a vehicular progression. A carriage, with horses and driver complete, he takes to be as simple a production of nature as a potato. But he is fond of sketching, and after breakfast, on the beautiful morning of Wednesday, the 21st, I persuaded him to walk out a mile or two and see a fragment of aqueduct ruin. It is a single glorious arch, buttressing the mountain-side upon the edge of a sharp descent to the valley of the Anio. The old road to Subiaco passes under it, and it is crowned by a crumbling tower built in the Middle Ages (whenever that was) against the Gaetani. While Storg sketched, I clambered. Below you, where the valley widens greenly toward other mountains, which the ripe Italian air distances with a bloom like that on unplucked grapes, are more arches, ossified arteries of what was once the heart of the world. Storg's sketch was highly approved of by Leopoldo, our guide, and by three or four peasants, who, being on their way to their morning's work in the fields, had, of course, nothing in particular to do, and stopped to see us see the ruin. Any one who has remarked how grandly the Romans do nothing will be slow to believe them an effete race. Their style is as the colossal to all other, and the name of Eternal City fits Rome also, because time is of no account in it. The Roman always waits as if he could afford it amply, and the slow centuries move quite fast enough for him. Time is to other races the field of a task-master, which they must painfully till; but to the Roman it is an entailed estate, which he enjoys and will transmit. The Neapolitan's laziness is that of a loafer; the Roman's is that of a noble. The poor Anglo-Saxon must count his hours, and look twice at his small change of quarters and minutes; but the Roman spends from a purse of Fortunatus. His *piccolo quarto d'ora* is like his *grosso*, a huge piece of copper, big enough for a shield, which stands only for a half-dime of our money. We poor fools of time always hurry as if we were the last type of man, the full stop with which Fate was closing the colophon of her volume, — as if we had just read in our newspaper, as we do of the banks on holidays, ☞ The world will close to-day at twelve o'clock, an hour earlier than usual. But the Roman is still an Ancient, with a vast future before him to tame and occupy. He and his ox and his plough are just as they were in Virgil's time or Ennius's. We beat him in many things; but in the impregnable fastness of his great rich nature he defies us.

We got back to Tivoli, — Storg affirming that he had walked fifteen miles. We saw the Temple of Cough, which is *not* the Temple of Cough, though it might have been a votive structure put up by some Tiburtine Dr. Wistar. We saw the villa of Mecænas, which is *not* the villa of Mecænas, and other equally satisfactory antiquities. All our English friends sketched the Citadel, of course, and one enthusiast attempted a likeness of the fall, which I unhappily mistook afterward for a semblance of the tail of one of the horses on the Monte Cavallo. Then we went to the Villa d' Este, famous on Ariosto's account, — and which Ariosto never saw. But the laurels were worthy to have made a chaplet for him, and the cypresses and the views were as fine as if he had seen them every day of his life.

Perhaps something I learned in going to see one of the gates of the town is more to the purpose, and may assist one in erecting the horoscope of *Italia Unita*. When Leopoldo first proposed to drag me through the mud to view this interesting piece of architecture, I demurred. But as he was very earnest about it, and as one seldom fails getting at a bit of character by submitting to one's guide, I yielded. Arrived at the spot, he put me at the best point of view, and said, —

" Behold, Lordship ! "

" I see nothing out of the common," said I.

" Lordship is kind enough here to look at a gate, the like of which exists not in all Italy, nay, in the whole world, — I speak not of England," for he thought me an *Inglese*.

" I am not blind, Leopoldo; where is the miracle ? "

" Here we dammed up the waters of the

Anio, first by artifice conducted to this spot, and letting them out upon the Romans, who stood besieging the town, drowned almost a whole army of them. (Lordship conceives?) They suspected nothing till they found themselves all torn to pieces at the foot of the hill yonder. (Lordship conceives?) *Eh! per Bacco!* we watered their porridge for them."

Leopoldo used *we* as Lord Buchan did *I*, meaning any of his ancestors.

" But tell me a little, Leopoldo, how many years is it since this happened ? "

" *Non saprei, signoria ;* it was in the antiquest times, certainly; but the Romans never come to our Fair, that we don't have blows about it, and perhaps a stab or two. Lordship understands ? "

I was quite repaid for my pilgrimage. I think I understand Italian politics better for hearing Leopoldo speak of the Romans, whose great dome is in full sight of Tivoli, as a foreign nation. But what perennial boyhood the whole story indicates!

Storg's sketch of the morning's ruin was so successful that I seduced him into a new expedition to the Ponte Sant' Antonio, another aqueduct arch about eight miles off. This was for the afternoon, and I succeeded the more easily, as we were to go on horseback. So I told Leopoldo to be at the gate of the Villa of Hadrian, at three o'clock, with three horses. Leopoldo's face, when I said three, was worth seeing; for the poor fellow had counted on nothing more than trotting beside our horses for sixteen miles, and getting half a dollar in the evening. Between doubt and hope, his face seemed to exude a kind of oil, which made it shine externally, after having first lubricated all the muscles inwardly.

"With *three* horses, Lordship?"

"Yes, *three*."

"Lordship is very sagacious. With *three* horses they go much quicker. It is finished, then, and they will have the kindness to find me at the gate with the beasts, at three o'clock precisely."

Leopoldo and I had compromised upon the term " Lordship." He had found me in the morning celebrating due rites before the Sibyl's Temple with strange incense of the nicotian herb, and had marked me for his prey. At the very high tide of sentiment, when the traveller lies with oyster-like openness in the soft ooze of reverie, do these parasitic crabs, the *ciceroni*, insert themselves as his inseparable bosom companions. Unhappy bivalve, lying so softly between thy two shells, of the actual and the possible, the one sustaining, the other widening above thee, till, oblivious of native mud, thou fanciest thyself a proper citizen only of the illimitable ocean which floods thee, — there is no escape! Vain are thy poor crustaceous efforts at self-isolation. The foe henceforth is a part of thy consciousness, thy landscape, and thyself, happy only if that irritation breed in thee the pearl of patience and of voluntary abstraction.

" Excellency wants a guide, very experienced, who has conducted with great mutual satisfaction many of his noble compatriots."

Puff, puff, and an attempt at looking as if I did not see him.

" Excellency will deign to look at my book of testimonials. When we return, Excellency will add his own.'

Puff, puff.

" Excellency regards the cascade, *præceps Anio*, as the good Horatius called it."

I thought of the *dissolve frigus* of the landlord in Roderick Random, and could not help smiling. Leopoldo saw his advantage.

" Excellency will find Leopoldo, when he shall choose to be ready."

" But I will positively not be called *Excellency*. I am not an ambassador, nor a very eminent Christian, and the phrase annoys me."

" To be sure, Excell— Lordship."

" I am an American."

" Certainly, an American, Lordship," — as if that settled the matter entirely. If I had told him I was a Caffre, it would have been just as clear to him. He surrendered the

"Excellency," but on general principles of human nature, I suppose, would not come a step lower than "Lordship." So we compromised on that. — P. S. It is wonderful how soon a republican ear reconciles itself with syllables of this description. I think *citizen* would find greater difficulties in the way of its naturalization, and as for *brother* — ah! well, in a Christian sense, certainly.

Three o'clock found us at the Villa of Hadrian. We had explored that incomparable ruin, and consecrated it, in the Homeric and Anglo-Saxon manner, by eating and drinking. Some of us sat in the shadow of one of the great walls, fitter for a city than a palace, over which a Nile of ivy, gushing from one narrow source, spread itself in widening inundations. A happy few listened to stories of Bagdad from Mrs. ——, whose silver hair gleamed, a palpable anachronism, like a snowfall in May, over that ever-youthful face, where the few sadder lines seemed but the signature of Age to a deed of quitclaim and release. Dear Tito, that exemplary traveller who never lost a day, had come back from renewed explorations, convinced by the eloquent *custode* that *Serapeion* was the name of an officer in the Prætorian Guard. I was explaining, in addition, that *Naumachia*, in the Greek tongue, signified a place artificially drained, when the horses were announced.

This put me to reflection. I felt, perhaps, a little as Mazeppa must, when told that his steed was at the door. For several years I had not been on the back of a horse, and was it not more than likely that these mountains might produce a yet more refractory breed of these ferocious animals than common? Who could tell the effect of grazing on a volcanic soil like that hereabout? I had vague recollections that the saddle nullified the laws governing the impulsion of inert bodies, exacerbating the centrifugal forces into a virulent activity, and proportionably narcotizing the centripetal. The phrase *ratio proportioned to the squares of the distances* impressed me with an awe which explained to me how the laws of nature had been of old personified and worshipped. Meditating these things, I walked with a cheerful aspect to the gate, where my saddled and bridled martyrdom awaited me.

"*Eccomi quà!*" said Leopoldo, hilariously. "Gentlemen will be good enough to select from the three best beasts in Tivoli."

"O, this one will serve me as well as any," said I, with an air of indifference, much as I have seen a gentleman help himself inadvertently to the best peach in the dish. I am not more selfish than becomes a Christian of the nineteenth century, but I looked on this as a clear case of *tabula in naufragio*, and had noticed that the animal in question had that tremulous droop of the lower lip which indicates senility, and the abdication of the wilder propensities. Moreover, he was the only one provided with a curb bit, or rather with two huge iron levers which might almost have served Archimedes for his problem. Our saddles were flat cushions covered with leather, brought by years of friction to the highest state of polish. Instead of a pommel, a perpendicular stake, about ten inches high, rose in front, which, in case of a stumble, would save one's brains, at the risk of certain evisceration. Behind, a glary slope invited me constantly to slide over the horse's tail. The selfish prudence of my choice had well-nigh proved the death of me, for this poor old brute, with that anxiety to oblige a *forestiero* which characterizes everybody here, could never make up his mind which of his four paces (and he had the rudiments of four — walk, trot, rack, and gallop) would be most agreeable to me. The period of transition is always unpleasant, and it was all transition. He treated me to a hodge-podge of all his several gaits at once. Saint Vitus was the only patron saint I could think of. My head jerked one way, my body another, while each of my legs became a pendulum vibrating furiously, one always forward while the other was back, so that I had all the appearance and all the labor of going afoot, and at the same time was bumped within an inch of my life. Waterton's alligator was nothing to it; it was like riding a hard-trotting armadillo bare-backed. There is a species of equitation peculiar to our native land, in which a rail from the nearest fence, with no preliminary incantation of *Horse and hattock!* is converted into a steed, and this alone may stand the comparison. Storg in the mean while was triumphantly taking the lead, his trousers working up very pleasantly above his knees, an insurrectionary movement which I also was unable to suppress in my own. I could bear it no longer.

"Le-e-o-o-p-o-o-o-l-l-l-d-d-o-o-o!" jolted I.

"Command, Lordship!" and we both came to a stop.

"It is necessary that we change horses immediately, or I shall be jelly."

"Certainly, Lordship"; and I soon had the pathetic satisfaction of seeing him subjected to all the excruciating experiments that had been tried upon myself. *Fiat experimentum in corpore vili*, thought his extempore lordship, Christopher Sly, to himself.

Meanwhile all the other accessories of our ride were delicious. It was a clear, cool day, and we soon left the high road for a bridle-path along the side of the mountain, among gigantic olive-trees, said to be five hundred years old, and which had certainly employed all their time in getting into the weirdest and wonderfullest shapes. Clearly in this green commonwealth there was no heavy roller of public opinion to flatten all character to a lawn-like uniformity. Everything was individual and eccentric. And there was something fearfully human, too, in the wildest contortions. It was some such wood that gave Dante the hint of his human forest in the seventh circle, and I should have dreaded to break a twig, lest I should hear that voice complaining,

"Perchè mi scerpi?
Non hai tu spirto di pietate alcuno?"

Our path lay along a kind of terrace, and at every opening we had glimpses of the billowy Campagna, with the great dome bulging from its rim, while on our right, changing ever as we rode, the Alban mountain showed us some new grace of that sweeping outline peculiar to volcanoes. At intervals the substructions of Roman villas would crop out from the soil like masses of rock, and deserving to rank as a geological formation by themselves. Indeed, in gazing into these dark caverns, one does not think of man more than at Staffa. Nature has adopted these fragments of a race who were dear to her. She has not suffered these bones of the great Queen to lack due sepulchral rites, but has flung over them the ceremonial handfuls of earth, and every year carefully renews the garlands of memorial flowers. Nay, if what they say in Rome be true, she has even made a new continent of the Colosseum, and given it a *flora* of its own.

At length, descending a little, we passed

through farm-yards and cultivated fields, where, from Leopoldo's conversations with the laborers, we discovered that he himself did not know the way for which he had undertaken to be guide. However, we presently came to our ruin, and very noble it was. The aqueduct had here been carried across a deep gorge, and over the little brook which wimpled along below towered an arch, as a bit of Shakespeare bestrides the exiguous rill of a discourse which it was intended to ornament. The only human habitation in sight was a little casetta on the top of a neighboring hill. What else of man's work could be seen was a ruined castle of the Middle Ages, and, far away upon the horizon, the eternal dome. A valley in the moon could scarce have been lonelier, could scarce have suggested more strongly the feeling of preteriteness and extinction. The stream below did not seem so much to sing as to murmur sadly, *Conclusum est; periisti!* and the wind, sighing through the arch, answered, *Periisti!* Nor was the silence of Monte Cavi without meaning. That cup, once full of fiery wine, in which it pledged Vesuvius and Ætna later born, was brimmed with innocent water now. Adam came upon the earth too late to see the glare of its last orgy, lighting the eyes of saurians in the reedy Campagna below. I almost fancied I could hear a voice like that which cried to the Egyptian pilot, *Great Pan is dead!* I was looking into the dreary socket where once glowed the eye that saw the whole earth vassal. Surely, this was the world's autumn, and I could hear the feet of Time rustling through the wreck of races and dynasties, cheap and inconsiderable as fallen leaves.

But a guide is not engaged to lead one into the world of imagination. He is as deadly to sentiment as a sniff of hartshorn. His position is a false one, like that of the critic, who is supposed to know everything, and expends himself in showing that he does not. If you should ever have the luck to attend a concert of the spheres, under the protection of an

Italian *cicerone*, he will expect you to listen to him rather than to it. He will say: " *Ecco, Signorìa*, that one in the red mantle is Signor Mars, eh! what a noblest *basso* is Signor Mars! but nothing (Lordship understands?) to what Signor Saturn used to be, (he with the golden belt, *Signorìa*,) only his voice is in ruins now, — scarce one note left upon another; but Lordship can see what it was by the remains, Roman remains, *Signorìa*, Roman remains, the work of giants. (Lordship understands?) They make no such voices now. Certainly, Signor Jupiter (with the yellow tunic, there) is a brave artist and a most sincere tenor; but since the time of the Republic " (if he think you an *oscurante*, or since the French, if he suspect you of being the least *red*) " we have no more good singing." And so on.

It is a well-known fact to all persons who are in the habit of climbing Jacob's-ladders, that, if any one speak to you during the operation, the fabric collapses, and you come some what uncomfortably to the ground. One can be hit with a remark, when he is beyond the reach of more material missiles. Leopoldo saw by my abstracted manner that I was getting away from him, and I was the only victim he had left, for Storg was making a sketch below. So he hastened to fetch me down again.

"Nero built this arch, Lordship." (He did n't, but Nero was Leopoldo's historical scapegoat.) "Lordship sees the dome? he will deign to look the least little to the left hand. Lordship has much intelligence. Well, Nero always did thus. His works always, always, had Rome in view."

He had already shown me two ruins, which he ascribed equally to Nero, and which could only have seen Rome by looking through a mountain. However, such trifles are nothing to an accomplished guide.

I remembered his quoting Horace in the morning.

"Do you understand Latin, Leopoldo?"

"I did a little once, Lordship. I went to the Jesuits' school at Tivoli. But what use of Latin to a *poverino* like me?"

"Were you intended for the church? Why did you leave the school?"

"Eh, Lordship!" and one of those shrugs which might mean that he left it of his own free will, or that he was expelled at point of toe. He added some contemptuous phrase about the priests.

"But, Leopoldo, you are a good Catholic?"

"Eh, Lordship, who knows? A man is no blinder for being poor, — nay, hunger sharpens the eyesight sometimes. The cardinals (their Eminences!) tell us that it is good to be poor, and that, in proportion as we lack on earth, it shall be made up to us in Paradise. Now, if the cardinals (their Eminences!) believe what they preach, why do they want to ride in such handsome carriages?"

"But are there many who think as you do?"

"Everybody, Lordship, but a few women and fools. What imports it what the fools think?"

An immense deal, I thought, an immense deal; for of what material is public opinion manufactured?

"Do you ever go to church?"

"Once a year, Lordship, at Easter, to mass and confession."

"Why once a year?"

"Because, Lordship, one must have a certificate from the priest. One might be sent to prison else, and one had rather go to confession than to jail. Eh, Lordship, it is a *porcheria*."

It is proper to add, that in what Leopoldo said of the priests he was not speaking of his old masters, the Jesuits. One never hears anything in Italy against the purity of their lives, or their learning and ability, though much against their unscrupulousness. Nor will any one who has ever enjoyed the gentle and dignified hospitality of the Benedictines be ready to believe any evil report of them.

By this time Storg had finished his sketch, and we remounted our grazing steeds. They were brisker as soon as their noses were turned homeward, and we did the eight miles back in an hour. The setting sun streamed through and among the Michael Angelesque olive-trunks, and, through the long colonnade of the bridle-path, fired the scarlet waistcoats and bodices of homeward villagers, or was sullenly absorbed in the long black cassock and flapped hat of a priest, who courteously saluted the strangers. Sometimes a mingled flock of sheep and goats (as if they had walked out of one of Claude's pictures) followed the shepherd, who, satyr-like, in goat-skin breeches, sang such songs as were acceptable before Tubal Cain struck out the laws of musical time from his anvil. The peasant, in his ragged brown cloak, or with blue jacket hanging from the left shoulder, still strides Romanly, — *incedit rex*, — and his eyes have a placid grandeur, inherited from those which watched the glittering snake of the Triumph, as it undulated along the Via Sacra. By his side moves with equal pace his woman-porter, the caryatid of a vast entablature of household-stuff, and learning in that harsh school a sinuous poise of body and a security of step beyond the highest snatch of the posture-master.

As we drew near Tivoli the earth was fast swinging into shadow. The darkening Campagna, climbing the sides of the nearer Monticelli in a gray belt of olive-spray, rolled on towards the blue island of Soracte, behind which we lost the sun. Yes, we had lost the sun; but in the wide chimney of the largest room at the Sibilla there danced madly, crackling with ilex and laurel, a bright ambassador from Sunland, Monsieur Le Feu, no pinchbeck substitute for his royal master. As we drew our chairs up, after the dinner due to Leopoldo's forethought, " Behold," said I, " the Resident of the great king near the court of our (this-day-created) **Hogan Moganships.**"

We sat looking into the fire, as it wavered from shining shape to shape of unearthliest fantasy, and both of us, no doubt, making out old faces among the embers, for we both said together, " Let us talk of old times."

" To the small hours," said the Edelmann ; "and instead of blundering off to Torneo to intrude chatteringly upon the midnight privacy of Apollo, let us promote the fire, there, to the rank of sun by brevet, and have a kind of undress rehearsal of those night wanderings of his here upon the ample stage of the hearth."

So we went through the whole catalogue of *Do you remembers?* and laughed at all the old stories, so dreary to an outsider. Then we grew pensive, and talked of the empty sockets in that golden band of our young friendship, — of S., with Grecian front, but unsevere, and Saxon M., to whom laughter was as natural as for a brook to ripple.

But Leopoldo had not done with us. We were to get back to Rome in the morning, and to that end must make a treaty with the company which ran the Tivoli diligence, the next day not being the regular period of departure for that prodigious structure. We had given Leopoldo twice his fee, and, setting a mean value upon our capacities in proportion, he expected to bag a neat percentage on our bargain. Alas! he had made a false estimate of the Arglo-Norman mind, which, capable of generosity as a compliment to itself, will stickle for the dust in the balance in a matter of business, and would blush at being *done* by Mercury himself.

Accordingly, at about nine o'clock there came a knock at the door, and, answering our *Favorisca!* in stalked Leopoldo, gravely followed by the two commissioners of the company.

" Behold me returned, Lordship, and these men are the *Vetturini*."

Why is it that men who have to do with

horses are the same all over Christendom? Is it that they acquire equine characteristics, or that this particular mystery is magnetic to certain sorts of men? Certainly they are marked unmistakably, and these two worthies would have looked perfectly natural in Yorkshire or Vermont. They were just alike, — *fortemque Gyan, fortemque Cloanthum,* — and you could not split an epithet between them. Simultaneously they threw back their large overcoats, and displayed spheroidal figures, over which the strongly pronounced stripes of their plaided waistcoats ran like parallels of latitude and longitude over a globe. Simultaneously they took off their hats and said, "Your servant, gentlemen." In Italy it is always necessary to make a *combinazione* beforehand about even the most customary matters, for there is no fixed *highest* price for anything. For a minute or two we stood reckoning each other's forces. Then I opened the first trench with the usual, " How much do you wish for carrying us to Rome at half past seven to-morrow morning?"

The enemy glanced, one at the other, and the result of this ocular *witenagemot* was that one said, " Four scudi, gentlemen."

The Edelmann Storg took his cigar from his mouth in order to whistle, and made a rather indecorous allusion to four gentlemen in the diplomatic service of his Majesty, the Prince of the Powers of the Air.

" Whe-ew! *quattro diavoli!* " said he.

"*Macehè!*" exclaimed I, attempting a flank-movement, " I had rather go on foot! " and threw as much horror into my face as if a proposition had been made to me to commit robbery, murder, and arson all together.

" For less than three scudi and a half the diligence parts not from Tivoli at an extraordinary hour," said the stout man, with an imperturbable gravity, intended to mask his retreat, and to make it seem that he was making the same proposal as at first.

Storg saw that they wavered, and opened upon them with his flying artillery of sarcasm.

"Do you take us for *Inglesi?* We are very well here, and will stay at the Sibilla," he sniffed scornfully.

"How much will Lordship give?" (This was showing the white feather.)

"Fifteen pauls," (a scudo and a half,) "*buonamano* included."

"It is impossible, gentlemen; for less than two scudi and a half the diligence parts not from Tivoli at an extraordinary hour."

"Fifteen pauls."

"Will Lordship give two scudi?" (with a slight flavor of mendicancy.)

"Fifteen pauls," (growing firm as we saw them waver.)

"Then, gentlemen, it is all over; it is impossible, gentlemen."

"Very good; a pleasant evening to you!" and they bowed themselves out.

As soon as the door closed behind them, Leopoldo, who had looked on in more and more anxious silence as the chance of plunder was whittled slimmer and slimmer by the sharp edges of the parley, saw instantly that it was for his interest to turn state's evidence against his accomplices.

"They will be back in a moment," he said knowingly, as if he had been of our side all along.

"Of course; we are aware of that." — It is always prudent to be aware of everything in travelling.

And, sure enough, in five minutes re-enter the stout men, as gravely as if everything had been thoroughly settled, and ask respectfully at what hour we would have the diligence.

This will serve as a specimen of Italian bargain-making. They do not feel happy if they get their first price. So easy a victory makes them sorry they had not asked twice as much, and, besides, they love the excitement of the contest. I have seen as much debate over a little earthen pot (value two cents) on the Ponte Vecchio, in Florence, as would have served for an operation of millions in the funds, the demand and the offer alternating so rapidly that the litigants might be supposed to be playing the ancient game of *morra*. It is a part of the universal fondness for gaming, and lotteries. An English gentleman once asked his Italian courier how large a percentage he made on all of his employer's money which passed through his hands. "About five per cent; sometimes more, sometimes less," was the answer. "Well, I will add that to your salary, in order that I may be rid of this uncomfortable feeling of being cheated." The courier mused a moment, and said, "But no, sir, I should not be happy; then it would not be sometimes more, sometimes less, and I should miss the excitement of the game."

22*d*. — This morning the diligence was at the door punctually, and, taking our seats in the *coupé*, we bade farewell to La Sibilla. But first we ran back for a parting glimpse at the water-fall. These last looks, like lovers' last kisses, are nouns of multitude, and presently the *povero stalliere, signori*, waited upon us cap in hand, telling us that the *vetturino* was impatient, and begging for drink-money in the same breath. Leopoldo hovered longingly afar, for these vultures respect times and seasons, and while one is fleshing his beak upon the foreign prey, the others forbear. The passengers in the diligence were not very lively. The Romans are a grave people, and more so than ever since '49. Of course, there was one priest among them. There always is; for the *mantis religiosa* is as inevitable to these public conveyances as the curculio is to the plum, and one could almost fancy that they were bred in the same way, — that the egg was inserted when the vehicle was green, became developed as it ripened, and never left it till it dropped withered from the pole. There was nothing noticeable on the road to Rome, except the strings of pack-horses and mules which we met returning with empty lime-sacks to Tivoli, whence comes the supply of Rome. A railroad was proposed, but the government would not allow it, because it would interfere with this carrying-trade, and wisely granted instead a charter for a road to Frascati, where there was no business whatever to be interfered with. About a mile of this is built in a style worthy of ancient Rome; and it is possible that eventually another mile may be accomplished, for some half-dozen laborers are at work upon it with wheelbarrows, in the leisurely Roman fashion. If it is ever finished, it will have nothing to carry but the conviction of its own uselessness. A railroad has been proposed to Civita Vecchia; but that is out of the question, because it would be profitable. On the whole, one does not regret the failure of these schemes. One would not approach the solitary emotion of a lifetime, such as is the first sight of Rome, at the rate of forty miles an hour. It is better, after painfully crawling up one of those long paved hills, to have the postilion turn in his saddle, and, pointing with his whip, (without looking, for he knows instinctively where it is,) say, *Ecco San Pietro!* Then you look tremblingly, and see it hovering visionary on the horizon's verge, and in a moment you are rattling and rumbling and wallowing down into the valley, and it is gone. So you play hide-and-seek with it all the rest of the way, and have time to converse with your sensations. You fancy you have got used to it at last; but from the next hill-top, lo, there it looms again, a new wonder, and you do not feel sure that it will keep its tryst till you find yourself under its shadow. The Dome is to Rome what Vesuvius is to Naples; only a greater wonder, for Michael Angelo hung it there. The traveller climbs it as he would a mountain, and finds the dwellings of men high up on its sacred cliffs. It has its annual eruption, too, at Easter, when the fire trickles and palpitates down its mighty shoulders, seen from far-off Tivoli. — No, the locomotive is less impertinent at Portici, hailing the imprisoned Titan there with a kindred shriek. Let it not vex the solemn Roman ghosts, or the nobly desolate Campagna, with whose solitudes the shattered vertebræ of the aqueducts are in truer sympathy.

24th. — To-day our journey to Subiaco properly begins. The jocund morning had called the beggars to their street-corners, and the women to the windows; the players of *morra* (a game probably as old as the invention of fingers), of chuck-farthing, and of bowls, had cheerfully begun the labors of the day; the plaintive cries of the chair-seaters, frog-venders, and certain other peripatetic merchants, the meaning of whose vocal advertisements I could never penetrate, quaver at regular intervals, now near and now far away; a solitary Jew with a sack over his shoulder, and who never is seen to stop, slouches along, every now and then croaking a penitential *Cenci!* as if he were somehow the embodied expiation (by some post-Ovidian metamorphosis) of that darkest Roman tragedy; women are bargaining for lettuce and endive; the slimy Triton in the Piazza Barberina spatters himself with vanishing diamonds; a peasant leads an ass on which sits the mother with the babe in her arms, — a living flight into Egypt; in short, the beautiful spring day had awakened all of Rome that can awaken yet (for the ideal Rome waits for another morning), when we rattled along in our *carrettella* on the way to Palestrina. A *carrettella* is to the perfected vehicle, as the coracle to the steamship; it is the first crude conception of a wheeled carriage. Doubtless the inventor of it was a prodigious genius in his day, and rode proudly in it, envied by the more fortunate pedestrian, and cushioned by his own inflated imagination. If the chariot of Achilles were like it, then was Hector happier at the tail than the son of Thetis on the box. It is an oblong basket upon two wheels, with a single seat rising in the middle. We had not jarred over a hundred yards of the Quattro Fontane, before we discovered that no elastic propugnaculum had been interposed between the body and the axle, so that we sat, as it were, on paving-stones, mitigated only by so much as well-seasoned ilex is less flinty-hearted than *tufo* or *breccia*. If there were any truth in the theory of developments, I am certain that we should have been furnished with a pair of rudimentary elliptical springs, at least, before half our day's journey was over. However, as one of those happy illustrations of ancient manners, which one meets with so often here, it was instructive; for I now clearly understand that it was not merely by reason of pomp that Hadrian used to be three days in getting to his villa, only twelve miles off. In spite of the author of " Vestiges," Nature, driven to extremities, can develop no more easy cushion than a blister, and no doubt treated an ancient emperor and a modern republican with severe impartiality.

It was difficult to talk without biting one's tongue; but as soon as we had got fairly beyond the gate, and out of sight of the last red-legged French soldier, and tightly-but toned *doganiere*, our driver became loquacious.

"I am a good Catnolic, — better than most," said he, suddenly.

"What do you mean by that?"

"Eh! they say Saint Peter wrought miracles, and there are enough who don't believe it; but *I* do. There's the Barberini Palace, — behold one miracle of Saint Peter! There's the Farnese, — behold another! There's the Borghese, — behold a third! But there's no end of them. No saint, nor all the saints put together, ever worked so many wonders as he; and then, *per Bacco!* he is the *uncle* of so many folks, — why, that's a miracle in itself, and of the greatest!"

Presently he added: "Do you know how we shall treat the priests when we make our next revolution? We shall treat them as they treat us, and that is after the fashion of the buffalo. For the buffalo is not content with getting a man down, but after that he gores him and thrusts him, always, always, as if he wished to cram him to the centre of the earth. Ah, if I were only keeper of hell-gate! Not a rascal of them all should ever get out into purgatory while I stood at the door!"

We remonstrated a little, but it only exasperated him the more.

"Blood of Judas! they will eat nothing else than gold, when a poor fellow's belly is as empty as San Lorenzo yonder. They'll have enough of it one of these days — but melted! How do you think they will like it for soup?"

Perhaps, if our vehicle had been blessed with springs, our vetturino would have been more placable. I confess a growing moroseness in myself, and a wandering speculation or two as to the possible fate of the builder of our chariot in the next world. But I am more and more persuaded every day, that, as far as the popular mind is concerned, Romanism is a dead thing in Italy. It survives only because there is nothing else to replace it with, for men must wear their old habits (however threadbare and out at the elbows) till they get better. It is literally a superstition, — a something left to *stand over* till the great commercial spirit of the nineteenth century balances his accounts again, and then it will be banished to the limbo of profit and loss. The Papacy lies dead in the Vatican, but the secret is kept for the present, and government is carried on in its name. After the fact gets abroad, perhaps its ghost will terrify men a little while longer, but only while they are in the dark, though the ghost of a creed is a hard thing to give a mortal wound to, and may be laid, after all, only in a Red Sea of blood.

So we rattled along till we came to a large *albergo* just below the village of Colonna. While our horse was taking his *rinfresco*, we climbed up to it, and found it desolate enough. — the houses never rebuilt since Consul Rienzi sacked it five hundred years ago. It was a kind of gray incrustation on the top of the hill, chiefly inhabited by pigs, chickens, and an old woman with a distaff, who looked as sacked and ruinous as everything around her. There she sat in the sun, a dreary, doting Clotho, who had outlived her sisters, and span endless destinies which none was left to cut at the appointed time. Of course she paused from her work a moment, and held out a skinny hand, with the usual, " Noblest gentlemen, give me something for charity." We gave her enough to pay Charon's ferriage across to her sisters, and departed hastily, for there was something uncanny about the place. In this climate even the finger-marks of Ruin herself are indelible, and the walls were still blackened with Rienzi's fires.

As we waited for our *carrettella*, I saw four or five of the lowest-looking peasants come up and read the handbill of a *tombola* (a kind of lottery) which was stuck up beside the inn-door. One of them read it aloud for our benefit, and with remarkable propriety of accent and emphasis. This benefit of clergy, however, is of no great consequence where there is nothing to read. In Rome, this morning, the walls were spattered with placards condemning the works of George Sand, Eugene Sue, Gioberti, and others. But in Rome one may contrive to read any book he likes; and I know Italians who are familiar with Swedenborg, and even Strauss.

Our stay at the *albergo* was illustrated by one other event, — a nightingale singing in a full-blossomed elder-bush on the edge of a brook just across the road. So liquid were the notes, and so full of spring, that the twig he tilted on seemed a conductor through which the mingled magnetism of brook and blossom flowed into him and were precipitated in music. Nature understands thoroughly the value of contrasts, and accordingly a donkey from a shed hard by, hitched and hesitated and agonized through his bray, so that we might be conscious at once of the positive and negative poles of song. It was pleasant to see with what undoubting enthusiasm he went through his solo, and vindicated Providence from the imputation of weakness in making such trifles as the nightingale yonder. "Give ear, O heaven and earth!" he seemed to say, "nor dream that good, sound common-sense is extinct or out of fashion so long as *I* live." I suppose Nature made the donkey half abstractedly, while she was feeling her way up to her ideal in the horse, and that his bray is in like manner an experimental sketch for the neigh of her finished animal.

We drove on to Palestrina, passing for some distance over an old Roman road, as carriageable as when it was built. Palestrina occupies the place of the once famous Temple of Fortune, whose ruins are perhaps a fitter monument of the fickle goddess than ever the perfect fane was.

> Come hither, weary ghosts that wail
>   O'er buried Nimroud's carven walls,
> And ye whose nightly footsteps frail
>   From the dread hush of Memphian halls
> Lead forth the whispering funerals!

Come hither, shade of ancient pain
   That, muffled sitting, hear'st the foam
To death-deaf Carthage shout in vain,
   And thou that in the Sibyl's tome
   Tear-stain'st the *never* after Rome!

Come, Marius, Wolsey, all ye great
   On whom proud Fortune stamped her heel,
And see herself the sport of Fate,
   Herself discrowned and made to feel
   The treason of her slippery wheel!

One climbs through a great part of the town by stone steps, passing fragments of Pelasgic wall, (for history, like geology, may be studied here in successive rocky *strata*,) and at length reaches the inn, called the *Cappellaro*, the sign of which is a great tin cardinal's hat, swinging from a small building on the other side of the street, so that a better view of it may be had from the hostelry itself. The landlady, a stout woman of about sixty years, welcomed us heartily, and burst forth into an eloquent eulogy on some fresh sea-fish which she had just received from Rome. She promised everything for dinner, leaving us to choose; but as a skilful juggler flitters the cards before you, and, while he seems to offer all, forces upon you the one he wishes, so we found that whenever we undertook to select from her voluble bill of fare, we had in some unaccountable manner always ordered sea-fish. Therefore, after a few vain efforts, we contented ourselves, and, while our dinner was cooking, climbed up to the top of the town. Here stands the deserted Palazzo Barberini, in which is a fine Roman mosaic pavement. It was a dreary old place. On the ceilings of some of the apartments were fading out the sprawling apotheoses of heroes of the family, (themselves long ago faded utterly,) who probably went through a somewhat different ceremony after their deaths from that represented here. One of the rooms on the ground-floor was still occupied, and from its huge grated windows there swelled and subsided at intervals a confused turmoil of voices, some talking, some singing, some swearing, and some lamenting, as if a page of Dante's Inferno had become suddenly alive under one's eye. This was the prison, and in front of each window a large stone block allowed *tête à-tête* discourses between the prisoners and their friends outside. Behind the palace rises a steep, rocky hill, with a continuation of ruined castle, the innocent fastness now of rooks and swallows. We walked down to a kind of terrace, and watched the Alban Mount (which saw the sunset for us by proxy) till the bloom trembled nearer and nearer to its summit, then went wholly out, we could not say when, and day was dead. Simultaneously we thought of dining, and clattered hastily down to the *Cappellaro*. We had to wait yet half an hour for dinner, and from where I sat I could see through the door of the dining-room a kind of large hall into which a door from the kitchen also opened. Presently I saw the landlady come out with a little hanging lamp in her hand, and seat herself amply before a row of baskets ranged upside-down along the wall. She carefully lifted the edge of one of these, and, after she had groped in it a moment, I heard that hoarse choking scream peculiar to fowls when seized by the leg in the dark, as if their throats were in their tibiæ after sunset. She took out a fine young cock and set him upon his feet before her, stupid with sleep, and blinking helplessly at the lamp, which he perhaps took for a sun in reduced circumstances, doubtful whether to crow or cackle. She looked at him admiringly, felt of him, sighed, gazed sadly at his coral crest, and put him back again. This ceremony she repeated with five or six of the baskets, and then went back into the kitchen. I thought of Thessalian hags and Arabian enchantresses, and wondered if these were transformed travellers, — for travellers go through queer transformations sometimes. Should Storg and I be crowing and scratching tomorrow morning, instead of going to Subiaco? Should we be Plato's men, with the feathers, instead of without them? I would probe this mystery. So, when the good woman came in to lay the table, I asked what she had been doing with the fowls.

"I thought to kill one for the gentlemen's soup; but they were so beautiful my heart failed me. Still, if the gentlemen wish it — only I thought two pigeons would be more delicate."

Of course we declined to be accessory to such a murder, and she went off delighted, returning in a few minutes with our dinner. First we had soup, then a roasted kid, then boiled pigeons, (of which the soup had been made,) and last the *pesci di mare*, which were not quite so great a novelty to us as to our good hostess. However, hospitality, like so many other things, is reciprocal, and the guest must bring his half, or it is naught. The prosperity of a dinner lies in the heart of him that eats it, and an appetite twelve miles long enabled us to do as great justice to the fish as if we were crowding all Lent into our meal. The landlady came and sat by us; a large and serious cat, winding her great tail around her, settled herself comfortably on the table, licking her paws now and then, with a poor relation's look at the fish; a small dog sprang into an empty chair, and a large one, with very confidential manners, would go from one to the other of us, laying his paw upon our arms as if he had an important secret to communicate, and alternately pricking and drooping his ears in hope or despondency. The *albergatrice* forthwith began to tell us her story, — how she was a widow, how she had borne thirteen children, twelve still living, and how she received a pension of sixty scudi a year, under the old Roman law, for her meritoriousness in this respect. The portrait of the son she had lost hung over the chimney-place, and, pointing to it, she burst forth into the following droll threnody. The remarks in parenthesis were screamed through the kitchen-door, which stood ajar, or addressed personally to us.

"O my son, my son! the doctors killed

him, just as truly as if they had poisoned him! O how beautiful he was! beautiful! *beautiful!!* BEAUTIFUL!!! (Are not those fish done yet?) Look, that is his likeness, — but he was handsomer. He was as big as that" (extending her arms), — " big breast, big shoulders, big sides, big legs! (Eat 'em, eat 'em, they won't hurt you, fresh sea-fish, fresh! *fresh!!* FRESH!!!) I told them the doctors had murdered him, when they carried him with torches! He had been hunting, and brought home some rabbits, I remember, for he was not one that ever came empty-handed, and got the fever, and you treated him for consumption, and killed him! (Shall I come out there, or will you bring some more fish?)" So she went on, talking to herself, to us, to the little *serva* in the kitchen, and to the medical profession in general, repeating every epithet three times, with increasing emphasis, till her voice rose to a scream, and contriving to mix up her living children with her dead one, the fish, the doctors, the *serva*, and the rabbits, till it was hard to say whether it was the fish that had large legs, whether the doctors had killed them, or the *serva* had killed the doctors, and whether the *bello! bello!! bello!!!* referred to her son or a particularly fine rabbit.

25th. — Having engaged our guide and horses the night before, we set out betimes this morning for Olevano. From Palestrina to Cavi the road winds along a narrow valley, following the course of a stream which rustles rather than roars below. Large chestnut-trees lean every way on the steep sides of the hills above us, and at every opening we could see great stretches of Campagna rolling away and away toward the bases of purple mountains streaked with snow. The sides of the road were drifted with heaps of wild hawthorn and honeysuckle in full bloom, and bubbling with innumerable nightingales that sang unseen. Overhead the sunny sky tinkled with larks, as if the frost in the air were breaking up and whirling away on the swollen currents of spring.

Before long we overtook a little old man hobbling toward Cavi, with a bag upon his back. This was the mail! Happy country, which Hurry and Worry have not yet subjugated! Then we clattered up and down the narrow paved streets of Cavi, through the market-place, full of men dressed all alike in blue jackets, blue breeches, and white stockings, who do not stare at the strangers, and so out at the farther gate. Now oftener and oftener we meet groups of peasants in gayest dresses, ragged pilgrims with staff and scallop, singing (horribly); then processions with bagpipes and pipes in front, droning and squealing (horribly); then strings of two-wheeled carts, eight or nine in each, and in the first the priest, book in hand, setting the stave, and all singing (horribly). This must be inquired into. Gigantic guide, who, splendid with blue sash and silver knee-buckles, has contrived, by incessant drumming with his heels, to get his mule in front, is hailed.

" Ho, Petruccio, what is the meaning of all this press of people ? "

" *Festa*, Lordship, at Genezzano."

" What *festa ?* "

" Of the Madonna, Lordship," and touches his hat, for they are all dreadfully afraid of her for some reason or other.

We are in luck, this being the great *festa* of the year among the mountains, — a thing which people go out of Rome to see.

" Where is Genezzano ? "

" Just over yonder, Lordship," and pointed to the left, where was what seemed like a monstrous crystallization of rock on the crown of a hill, with three or four taller crags of castle towering in the midst, and all gray, except the tiled roofs, whose wrinkled sides were gold-washed with a bright yellow lichen, as if ripples, turned by some spell to stone, had contrived to detain the sunshine with which they were touched at the moment of transformation.

The road, wherever it came into sight,

burned with brilliant costumes, like an illuminated page of Froissart. Gigantic guide meanwhile shows an uncomfortable and fidgety reluctance to turn aside and enter fairyland, which is wholly unaccountable. Is the huge earthen creature an Afrite, under sacred pledge to Solomon, and in danger of being sealed up again, if he venture near the festival of our Blessed Lady ? If so, *that* also were a ceremony worth seeing, and we insist. He wriggles and swings his great feet with an evident impulse to begin kicking the sides of his mule again and fly. The way over the hills from Genezzano to Olevano he pronounces *seomodissima*, demanding of every peasant who goes by if it be not entirely impassable. This leading question, put in all the tones of plausible entreaty he can command, meets the invariable reply, " *È scomoda, davvero ; ma per le bestie — eh !* " (it is bad, of a truth, but for the beasts — eh !) and then cne of those indescribable shrugs, unintelligible at first as the compass to a savage, but in which the expert can make twenty hair's-breadth distinctions between N. E. and N. N. E.

Finding that destiny had written it on his forehead, the guide at last turned and went cantering and kicking toward Genezzano, we following. Just before you reach the town, the road turns sharply to the right, and, crossing a little gorge, loses itself in the dark gateway. Outside the gate is an open space, which formicated with peasantry in every variety of costume that was *not* Parisian. Laughing women were climbing upon their horses (which they bestride like men); pilgrims were chanting, and beggars (the howl of an Italian beggar in the country is something terrible) howling in discordant rivalry. It was a scene lively enough to make Heraclitus shed a double allowance of tears; but our giant was still discomforted. As soon as we had entered the gate, he dodged into a little back-street, just as we were getting out of which the mystery of his unwillingness was cleared up. He had been endeavoring to avoid a creditor. But it so chanced (as Fate can hang a man with even a rope of sand) that the enemy was in position just at the end of this very lane, where it debouched into the Piazza of the town.

The disputes of Italians are very droll things, and I will accordingly bag the one which is now imminent, as a specimen. They quarrel as unaccountably as dogs, who put their noses together, dislike each other's kind of smell, and instantly tumble one over the other, with noise enough to draw the eyes of a whole street. So these people burst out, without apparent preliminaries, into a noise and fury and war-dance which would imply the very utmost pitch and agony of exasperation. And the subsidence is as sudden. They explode each other on mere contact, as if by a law of nature, like two hostile gases. They do not grow warm, but leap at once from zero to some degree of white-heat, to indicate which no Anglo-Saxon thermometer of wrath is highly enough graduated. If I were asked to name one universal characteristic of an Italian town, I should say, two men clamoring and shaking themselves to pieces at each other, and a woman leaning lazily out of a window, and perhaps looking at something else. Till one gets used to this kind of thing, one expects some horrible catastrophe; but during eight months in Italy I have only seen blows exchanged thrice. In the present case the explosion was of harmless gunpowder.

"Why-haven't-you-paid-those-fifty-five-bajocchi-at-the-*pizzicarolo's?*" began the adversary, speaking with such inconceivable rapidity that he made only one word, nay, as it seemed, one monosyllable, of the whole sentence. Our giant, with a controversial genius which I should not have suspected in him, immediately, and with great adroitness, changed the ground of dispute, and, instead of remaining an insolvent debtor, raised himself at once to the ethical position of a moralist, resisting an unjust demand from principle.

"It was only *forty*-five," roared he.

"But I say *fifty*-five," screamed the other, and shook his close-cropped head as a boy does an apple on the end of a switch, as if he meant presently to jerk it off at his antagonist.

"*Birbone!*" yelled the guide, gesticulating so furiously with every square inch of his ponderous body that I thought he would throw his mule over, the poor beast standing all the while with drooping head and ears while the thunders of this man-quake burst over him. So feels the tortoise that sustains the globe when earth suffers fiery convulsions.

"*Birbante!*" retorted the creditor, and the opprobrious epithet clattered from between his shaking jaws as a refractory copper is rattled out of a Jehoiada-box by a child.

"*Andate vi far friggere!*" howled giant.

"*Andate ditto, ditto!*" echoed creditor, — and behold, the thing is over! The giant promises to attend to the affair when he comes back, the creditor returns to his booth, and we ride on.

Speaking of Italian quarrels, I am tempted to parenthesize here another which I saw at Civita Vecchia. We had been five days on our way from Leghorn in a French steamer, a voyage performed usually, I think, in about thirteen hours. It was heavy weather, blowing what a sailor would call half a gale of wind, and the caution of our captain, not to call it fear, led him to put in for shelter first at Porto Ferrajo in Elba, and then at Santo Stefano on the Italian coast. Our little black water-beetle of a mail-packet *was* knocked about pretty well, and all the Italian passengers disappeared in the forward cabin before we were out of port. When we were fairly at anchor within the harbor of Civita Vecchia, they crawled out again, sluggish as winter flies, their vealy faces mezzotinted with soot. One of them presently appeared in the custom-house, his only luggage being a cage closely covered with a dirty red handkerchief, which represented his linen.

"What have you in the cage?" asked the *doganiere*.

"Eh! nothing other than a parrot."

"There is a duty of one scudo and one bajoccho, then."

"*Santo diavolo!* but what hoggishness!"

Thereupon instant and simultaneous blow-up, or rather a series of explosions, like those in honor of a Neapolitan saint's-day, lasting about ten minutes, and followed by as sudden quiet. In the course of it, the owner of the bird, playing irreverently on the first half of its name (*papp*agallo), hinted that it would be a high duty for his Holiness himself (*Papa*). After a pause for breath, he said quietly, as if nothing had happened, "Very good, then, since I must pay, I will," and began fumbling for the money.

"Meanwhile, do me the politeness to show me the bird," said the officer.

"With all pleasure," and, lifting a corner of the handkerchief, there lay the object of dispute on his back, stone-dead, with his claws curled up helplessly on each side his breast. I believe the owner would have been pleased had it even been his grandmother who had thus evaded duty, so exquisite is the pleasure of an Italian in escaping payment of anything.

"I make a present of the poor bird," said he blandly.

The publican, however, seemed to feel that he had been somehow cheated, and I left them in high debate, as to whether the bird were dead when it entered the custom-house, and, if it had been, whether a dead parrot were dutiable. Do not blame me for being entertained and trying to entertain you with these trifles. I remember Virgil's stern

"Che per poco è che teco non mi risso,"

but Dante's journey was of more import to himself and others than mine.

I am struck by the freshness and force of the passions in Europeans, and cannot help feeling as if there were something healthy in it. When I think of the versatile and accommodating habits of America, it seems like a land without thunder-storms. In proportion as man grows commercial, does he also become dispassionate and incapable of electric emotions? The driving-wheels of all-powerful nature are in the back of the head, and, as man is the highest type of organization, so a nation is better or worse as it advances toward the highest type of man, or recedes from it. But it is ill with a nation when the cerebrum sucks the cerebellum dry, for it cannot live by intellect alone. The broad foreheads always carry the day at last, but only when they are based on or buttressed with massive hind-heads. It would be easier to make a people great in whom the animal is vigorous, than to keep one so after it has begun to spindle into over-intellectuality. The hands that have grasped dominion and held it have been large and hard; those from which it has slipped, delicate, and apt for the lyre and the pencil. Moreover, brain is always to be bought, but passion never comes to market. On the whole, I am rather inclined to like this European impatience and fire, even while I laugh at it, and sometimes find myself surmising whether a people who, like the Americans, put up quietly with all sorts of petty personal impositions and injustices, will not at length find it too great a bore to quarrel with great public wrongs.

Meanwhile, I must remember that I am in Genezzano, and not in the lecturer's desk. We walked about for an hour or two, admiring the beauty and grand bearing of the women, and the picturesque vivacity and ever-renewing unassuetude of the whole scene. Take six of the most party-colored dreams, break them to pieces, put them into a fantasy-kaleidoscope, and when you look through it you will see something that for strangeness, vividness, and mutability looked like the little Piazza of Genezzano seen from the church porch. As we wound through the narrow streets again to the stables where we had left our horses, a branch of laurel or ilex would mark a wine-shop, and, looking till our eye cooled and toned itself down to dusky sympathy with the crypt, we could see the smoky interior sprinkled with white head-cloths and scarlet bodices, with here and there a yellow spot of lettuce or the red inward gleam of a wine-flask. The head-dress is precisely of that most ancient pattern seen on Egyptian statues, and so colossal are many of the wearers, that you might almost think you saw a party of young sphinxes carousing in the sunless core of a pyramid.

We remounted our beasts, and, for about a mile, cantered gayly along a fine road, and then turned into a by-path along the flank of a mountain. Here the guide's *strada scomodissima* began, and we were forced to dismount, and drag our horses downward for a mile or two. We crossed a small plain in the valley, and then began to climb the opposite ascent. The path was perhaps four feet broad, and was paved with irregularly shaped blocks of stone, which, having been raised and lowered, tipped, twisted, undermined, and generally capsized by the rains and frosts of centuries, presented the most diabolically ingenious traps and pit-falls. All the while the scenery was beautiful. Mountains of every shape and hue changed their slow outlines ever as we moved, now opening, now closing around us, sometimes peering down solemnly at us over each other's shoulders, and then sinking slowly out of sight, or, at some sharp turn of the path, seeming to stride into the valley and confront us with their craggy challenge, — a challenge which the little valleys accepted, if we did not, matching their rarest tints of gray and brown, and pink and purple, or that royal dye to make which all these were profusely melted together for a moment's ornament, with as many shades of various green and yellow. Gray towns crowded and clung on the tops of peaks that seemed inaccessible. We owe a great deal of picturesqueness to the quarrels and thieveries of the barons of the Middle Ages. The traveller and artist should put up a prayer for their battered old souls. I was to be out of their way and that of the Saracens that people were driven to make their homes in spots so sublime and inconvenient that the eye alone finds it pleasant to climb up to them. Nothing else but an American land-company ever managed to induce settlers upon territory of such uninhabitable quality. I have seen an insect that makes a mask for himself out of the lichens of the rock over which he crawls, contriving so to deceive the birds; and the towns in this wild region would seem to have been built on the same principle. Made of the same stone with the cliffs on which they perch, it asks good eyesight to make them out at the distance of a few miles, and every wandering mountain-mist annihilates them for the moment.

At intervals, I could hear the giant, after digging at the sides of his mule with his spurless heels, growling to himself, and imprecating an apoplexy (*accidente*) upon the path and him who made it. This is the universal malediction here, and once it was put into rhyme for my benefit. I was coming down the rusty steps of San Gregorio one day, and having paid no heed to a stout woman of thirty odd who begged somewhat obtrusively, she screamed after me,

> "Ah, vi pigli un accidente,
> Voi che non date niente!"

> Ah, may a sudden apoplexy,
> You who give not, come and vex ye!

Our guide could not long appease his mind with this milder type of objurgation, but soon intensified it into *accidentaccio*, which means a selected apoplexy of uncommon size and ugliness. As the path grew worse and worse, so did the repetition of this phrase (for he was slow of invention) become more frequent, till at last he did nothing but kick and curse, mentally, I have no doubt, including us in his malediction. I think it would have gratified Longinus r Fuseli (both of whom commended swearing) to have heard him. Before long we turned the flank of the hill by a little shrine of the Madonna, and there was Olevano just above us. Like the other towns in this district, it was the diadem of an abrupt peak of rock. From the midst of it jutted the ruins of an old stronghold of the Colonna. Probably not a house has been built in it for centuries. To enter the town, we literally rode up a long flight of stone steps, and soon found ourselves in the Piazza. We stopped to buy some cigars, and the *zigararo*, as he rolled them up, asked if we did not want dinner. We told him we should get it at the inn. *Benissimo*, he would be there before us. What he meant, we could not divine; but it turned out that he was the landlord, and that the inn only became such when strangers arrived, relapsing again immediately into a private dwelling. We found our host ready to receive us, and went up to a large room on the first floor. After due instructions, we seated ourselves at the open windows,—Storg to sketch, and I to take a mental calotype of the view. Among the many lovely ones of the day, this was the loveliest, — or was it only that the charm of repose was added? On our right was the silent castle, and beyond it the silent mountains. To the left we looked down over the clustering houses upon a campagna-valley of peaceful cultivation, vineyards, olive-orchards, grain-fields in their earliest green, and dark stripes of new-ploughed earth, over which the cloud-shadows melted tracklessly toward the hills which round softly upward to Monte Cavi.

When our dinner came, and with it a flask of drowsy red Aleatico, like ink with a suspicion of life-blood in it, such as one might fancy Shakespeare to have dipped his quill in, we had our table so placed that the satisfaction of our hunger might be dissensualized by the view from the windows. Many a glutton has eaten up farms and woodlands and pastures, and so did we, æsthetically, saucing our *frittata* and flavoring our Aleatico with landscape. It is a fine thing when we can accustom our animal appetites to good society, when body and soul (like master and servant in an Arab tent) sit down together at the same board. This thought is forced upon one very often in Italy, as one picnics in enchanted spots, where Imagination and Fancy play the parts of the unseen waiters in the fairy-story, and serve us with course after course of their ethereal dishes. Sense is satisfied with less and simpler food when sense and spirit are fed together, and the feast of the loaves and fishes is spread for us anew. If it be important for a state to educate its lower classes, so is it for us personally to instruct, elevate, and refine our senses, the lower classes of our private body-politic, and which, if left to their own brute instincts, will disorder or destroy the whole commonwealth with flaming insurrection.

After dinner came our guide to be paid. He, too, had had his *frittata* and his *fiasco* (or two), and came back absurdly comic, reminding one of the giant who was so taken in by the little tailor. He was not in the least tipsy; but the wine had excited his poor wits, whose destiny it was (awkward servants as they were!) to trip up and tumble over each other in proportion as they became zealous. He was very anxious to *do* us in some way or other; he only vaguely guessed how, but felt so gigantically good-natured that he could not keep his face sober long enough. It is quite clear why the Italians have no word but *recitare* to express acting, for their stage is no more theatric than their street, and to exaggerate in the least would be ridiculous. We graver-tempered and -mannered Septentrions must give the pegs a screw or two to bring our spirits up to nature's concert-pitch. Stcrg and I sat enjoying the exhibition of our giant, as if we had no more concern in it than as a comedy. It was nothing but a spectacle to us, at which we were present as critics, while he inveighed, expostulated, argued, and besought, in a breath. Finding all his attempts miscarry, or resulting in nothing more solid than applause, he said, "*Forse non capiscono?*"

(Perhaps you don't understand?) "*Capiscono pur' troppo,*" (They understand only too well,) replied the landlord, upon which *terræ filius* burst into a laugh, and began begging for more *buonamano*. Failing in this, he tightened his sash, offered to kiss our lordships' hands, an act of homage which we declined, and departed, carefully avoiding Genezzano on his return, I make no doubt.

We paid our bill, and went down to the door, where we found our guides and donkeys, the host's handsome wife and handsomer daughter, with two of *her* daughters, and a crowd of women and children waiting to witness the *exit* of the foreigners. We made all the mothers and children happy by a discriminating *largesse* of copper among the little ones. They are a charming people, the natives of these out-of-the-way Italian towns, if kindness, courtesy, and good looks make people charming. Our beards and felt hats, which make us pass for artists, were our passports to the warmest welcome and the best cheer everywhere. Reluctantly we mounted our donkeys, and trotted away, our guides (a man and a boy) running by the flank (true henchmen, haunchmen, *flanquiers* or flunkeys) and inspiring the little animals with pokes in the side, or with the even more effectual *ahrrrrrrr!* Is there any radical affinity between this rolling fire of *r*'s and the word *arra*, which means hansel or earnest-money? The sound is the same, and has a marvellous spur-power over the donkey, who seems to understand that full payment of goad or cudgel is to follow. I have known it to move even a Sicilian mule, the least sensitive and most obstinate of creatures with ears, except a British church-warden.

We wound along under a bleak hill, more desolate than anything I had ever seen. The old gray rocks seemed not to thrust themselves out of the rusty soil, but rather to be stabbed into it, as if they had been hailed down upon it by some volcano. There was nearly as much look of design as there is in a druidical circle and the whole looked like some graveyard in an extinguished world, the monument of mortality itself, such as Bishop Wilkins might have found in the moon, if he had ever got thither. The path grew ever wilder, and Rojate, the next town we came to, grim and grizzly, under a grim and grizzly sky of low-trailing clouds, which had suddenly gathered, looked drearier even than the desolations we had passed. It was easy to understand why rocks should like to live here well enough; but what could have brought men hither, and then kept them here, was beyond all reasonable surmise. Barren hills stood sullenly aloof all around, incapable of any crop but lichens.

We entered the gate, and found ourselves in the midst of a group of wild-looking men gathered about the door of a wine-shop. Some of them were armed with long guns, and we saw (for the first time *in situ*) the tall bandit hat with ribbons wound round it, — such as one is familiar with in operas, and on the heads of those inhabitants of the *Scali-*

nata in Rome, who have a costume of their own, and placidly serve as models through the whole pictorial range of divine and human nature, from the *Padre Eterno* to Judas. Twenty years ago, when my notion of an Italian was divided between a monk and a bravo, the first of whom did nothing but enter at secret doors and drink your health in poison, while the other lived behind corners, supporting himself by the productive industry of digging your person all over with a stiletto, I should have looked for instant assassination from these carousing ruffians. But the only blood shed on the occasion was that of the grape. A ride over the mountains for two hours had made us thirsty, and two or three bajocchi gave a tumbler of *vino asciutto* to all four of us. "You are welcome," said one of the men, "we are all artists after a fashion; we are all brothers." The manners here are more republican, and the title of *lordship* disappears altogether. Another came up and insisted that we should drink a second flask of wine as his guests. In vain we protested; no artist should pass through Rojate without accepting that token of good-will, and with the liberal help of our guides we contrived to gulp it down. He was for another; but we protested that we were entirely full, and that it was impossible. I dare say the poor fellow would have spent a week's earnings on us, if we would have allowed it. We proposed to return the civility, and to leave a paul for them to drink a good journey to us after we were gone; but they would not listen to it. Our entertainer followed us along to the Piazza, begging one of us to let him serve as donkey-driver to Subiaco. When this was denied, he said that there was a *festa* here also, and that we must stop long enough to see the procession of *zitelle* (young girls), which would soon begin. But evening was already gathering, the clouds grew momently darker, and fierce, damp gusts, striking us with the suddenness of a blow, promised a wild night. We had still eight miles of mountain-path before us, and we struggled away. As we crossed the next summit beyond the town, a sound of chanting drifted by us on the wind, wavered hither and thither, now heard, now lost, then a doubtful something between song and gust, and, lingering a few moments, we saw the white head-dresses, gliding two by two, across a gap between the houses. The scene and the music were both in neutral tints, a sketch, as it were, in *sepia* a little blurred.

Before long the clouds almost brushed us as they eddied silently by, and then it began to rain, first mistily, and then in thick, hard drops. Fortunately there was a moon, shining placidly in the desert heaven above all this turmoil, or we could not have found our path, which in a few moments became a roaring torrent almost knee-deep. It was a cold rain, and far above us, where the mountain-peaks tore gaps in the clouds, we could see the white silence of new-fallen snow. Sometimes we had to dismount and wade, — a cir cumstance which did not make our saddles more comfortable when we returned to them and could hear them go *crosh, crosh*, as the water gurgled out of them at every jolt. There was no hope of shelter nearer than Subiaco, no sign of man, and no sound but the multitudinous roar of waters on every side. Rivulet whispered to rivulet, and water-fall shouted to water-fall, as they leaped from rock to rock, all hurrying to reinforce the main torrent below, which hummed onward toward the Anio with dilated heart. So gathered the hoarse Northern swarms to descend upon sunken Italy; and so forever does physical and intellectual force seek its fatal equilibrium, rushing in and occupying wherever it is drawn by the attraction of a lower level.

We forded large streams that had been dry beds an hour before; and so sudden was the creation of the floods, that it gave one almost as fresh a feeling of water as if one had been present in Eden when the first rock gave birth to the first fountain. I had a severe cold, I was wet through from the hips downward, and yet I never enjoyed anything more in my life, — so different is the shower-bath to which we doom ourselves from that whose string is pulled by the prison-warden compulsion. After our little bearers had tottered us up and down the dusky steeps of a few more mountain-spurs, where a misstep would have sent us spinning down the fathomless black nowhere below, we came out upon the highroad, and found it a fine one, as all the great Italian roads are. The rain broke off suddenly, and on the left, seeming about half a mile away, sparkled the lights of Subiaco, flashing intermittently like a knot of fire-flies in a meadow. The town, owing to the necessary windings of the road, was still three miles off, and just as the guides had progued and *ahrred* the donkeys into a brisk joggle, I resolved to give up my saddle to the boy, and try Tom Coryate's compasses. It was partly out of numanity to myself and partly to him, for he was tired and I was cold. The elder guide and I took the lead, and, as I looked back, I laughed to see the lolling ears of Storg's donkey thrust from under his long cloak, as if he were coming out from a black Arab tent. We soon left them behind, and paused at a bridge over the Anio till we heard the patter of little hoofs again. The bridge is a single arch, bent between the steep edges of a gorge through which the Anio huddled far below, showing a green gleam here and there in the struggling moonlight, as if a fish rolled up his burnished flank. After another mile and a half, we reached the gate, and awaited our companions. It was dreary enough, — waiting always is, — and as the snow-chilled wind whistled through the damp archway where we stood, my legs illustrated feelingly to me how they cool water in the East, by wrapping the jars with wet woollen, and setting them in a draught. At last they came; I remounted, and we went sliding through the steep, wet streets till we had fairly passed through the whole town. Before a long building of two stories, without a symptom of past or future light, we stopped. "*Ecco la Paletta!*" said the guide, and began to pound furiously on the door with a large stone, which he some time before had provided for the purpose. After a long period of sullen irresponsiveness, we heard descending footsteps, light streamed through the chinks of the door, and the invariable "*Chi è?*" which precedes the unbarring of all portals here, came from within. "*Due forestieri,*" answered the guide, and the bars rattled in hasty welcome. "Make us," we exclaimed, as we stiffly climbed down from our perches, "your biggest fire in your biggest chimney, and then we will talk of supper!" In five minutes two great laurel-fagots were spitting and crackling in an enormous fireplace; and Storg and I were in the costume which Don Quixote wore on the Brown Mountain. Of course there was nothing for supper but a *frittata;* but there are worse things in the world than a *frittata col prosciutto,* and we discussed it like a society just emerging from barbarism, the upper half of our persons presenting all the essentials of an advanced civilization, while our legs skulked under the table as free from sartorial impertinences as those of the noblest savage that ever ran wild in the woods. And so *eccoci finalmente arrivati!*

27th. — Nothing can be more lovely than the scenery about Subiaco. The town itself is built on a kind of cone rising from the midst of a valley abounding in olives and vines, with a superb mountain horizon around it, and the green Anio cascading at its feet. As you walk to the high-perched convent of San Benedetto, you look across the river on your right just after leaving the town, to a cliff over which the ivy pours in torrents, and in which dwellings have been hollowed out. In the black doorway of every one sits a woman in scarlet bodice and white head-gear, with a distaff, spinning, while overhead countless nightingales sing at once from the fringe of shrubbery. The glorious great white clouds look over the mountain-tops into our enchanted valley, and sometimes a lock of their vapory wool would be torn off, to lie for a while in some inaccessible ravine like a snow-drift; but it seemed as if no shadow could fly over our privacy of sunshine to-day. The approach to the monastery is delicious. You pass out of the hot sun into the green shadows of ancient ilexes, leaning and twisting every way that is graceful, their branches velvety with brilliant moss, in which grow feathery ferns, fringing them with a halo of verdure. Then comes the convent, with its pleasant old monks, who show their sacred vessels (one by Cellini) and their relics, among which is a finger-bone of one of the Innocents. Lower down is a convent of Santa Scolastica, where the first book was printed in Italy.

But though one may have daylight till after twenty-four o'clock in Italy, the days are no longer than ours, and I must go back to La Paletta to see about a *vettura* to Tivoli. I leave Storg sketching, and walk slowly down, lingering over the ever-changeful views, lingering opposite the nightingale-cliff, but get back to Subiaco and the *vetturino* at last. The growl of a thunder-storm soon brought Storg home, and we leave Subiaco triumphantly, at five o'clock, in a light carriage, drawn by three gray stallions (harnessed abreast) on the full gallop. I cannot describe our drive, the mountain-towns, with their files of girls winding up from the fountain with balanced water-jars of ruddy copper, or chattering around it bright-hued as parrots, the ruined castles, the green gleams of the capricious river, the one great mountain that soaked up all the rose of sunset, and, after all else grew dim, still glowed as if with inward fires, and, later, the white spray smoke of Tivoli that drove down the valley under a clear cold moon, contrasting strangely with the red glare of the lime-furnace on the opposite hillside. It is well that we can be happy sometimes without peeping and botanizing in the materials that make us so. It is not ofter that we can escape the evil genius of analysis that haunts our modern daylight of self-consciousness (*wir haben ja aufgeklärt!*) and enjoy a day of right Chaucer.

P. S. Now that I am printing this, a dear friend sends me an old letter, and says, "Slip in somewhere, by way of contrast, what you wrote me of your visit to Passawampscot." It is odd, almost painful, to be confronted with your past self and your past self's doings, when you have forgotten both. But here is my bit of American scenery, such as it is.

While we were waiting for the boat, we had time to investigate P. a little. We wandered about with no one to molest us or make us afraid. No *cicerone* was lying in wait for us, no verger expected with funeral solemnity the more than compulsory shilling. I remember the whole population of Cortona gathering round me, and beseeching me not to leave their city till I had seen the *lampadone*, whose keeper had unhappily gone out to walk, taking the key with him. Thank Fortune, here were no antiquities, no galleries of Pre-Raphaelite art, every lank figure looking as if it had been stretched on a rack, before which the Anglo-Saxon writhes because he ought to like them and cannot for the soul of him. It is a pretty little village, cuddled down among the hills, the clay soil of which gives them, to a pilgrim from the parched gravelly inland, a look of almost fanatical green. The fields are broad, and wholly given up to the grazing of cattle and sheep, which dotted them thickly in the breezy sunshine. The open doors of a barn, through which the wind flowed rustling the loose locks of the mow, attracted us. Swallows swam in and out with level wings, or crossed each other, twittering in the dusky mouth of their hay-scented cavern. Two or three hens and a cock (none of your gawky Shanghais, long-legged as a French peasant on his stilts, but the true red cock of the ballads, full-chested, coral-combed, fountain tailed) were inquiring for hay-seed in the background.

What frame in what gallery ever enclosed such a picture as is squared within the groundsel, side-posts, and lintel of a barn-door, whether for eye or fancy? The shining floor suggests the flail-beat of autumn, that pleasantest of monotonous sounds, and the later husking-bee, where the lads and lasses sit round laughingly busy under the swinging lantern.

Here we found a fine, stalwart fellow shearing sheep. This was something new to us, and we watched him for some time with many questions, which he answered with off-hand good-nature. Going away, I thanked him for having taught me something. He laughed, and said, "Ef you 'll take off them gloves o' yourn, I 'll give ye a try at the practical part on 't." He was in the right of it. I never saw anything handsomer than those brown hands of his, on which the sinews stood out as he handled his shears, tight as a drawn bow-string. How much more admirable is this tawny vigor, the badge of fruitful toil, than the crop of early muscle that heads out under the forcing-glass of the gymnasium! Foreigners do not feel easy in America, because there are no peasants and underlings here to be humble to them. The truth is, that none but those who feel themselves only artificially the superiors of our sturdy yeomen see in their self-respect any uncomfortable *assumption* of equality. It is the last thing the yeoman is likely to think of. They do not like the " I say, ma good fellah " kind of style, and commonly contrive to snub it. They do not value condescension at the same rate that he does who vouchsafes it to them. If it be a good thing for an English duke that he has no social superiors, I think it can hardly be bad for a Yankee farmer. If it be a bad thing for the duke that he meets none but inferiors, it cannot harm the farmer much that he never has the chance. At any rate, there was no thought of incivility in my friend Hobbinol's jibe at my kids, only a kind of jolly superiority. But I did not like to be taken for a city *gent*, so I told him I was born and bred in the country as well as he. He laughed again, and said, "Wal, anyhow, I've the advantage of ye, for you never see a sheep shore, an' I've ben to the Opery and shore sheep myself into the bargain." He told me that there were two hundred sheep in the town, and that his father could remember when there were four times as many. The sea laps and mumbles the soft roots of the hills, and licks away an acre or two of good pasturage every season. The father, an old man of eighty, stood looking on, pleased with his son's wit, and brown as if the Passawampscot fogs were walnut-juice.

We dined at a little tavern, with a gilded ball hung out for sign, — a waif, I fancy, from some shipwreck. The landlady was a brisk, amusing little body, who soon informed us that her husband was own cousin to a Senator of the United States. A very elaborate sampler in the parlor, in which an obelisk was wept over by a somewhat costly willow in silver thread, recorded the virtues of the Senator's maternal grandfather and grandmother. After dinner, as we sat smoking our pipes on the piazza, our good hostess brought her little daughter, and made her repeat verses utterly unintelligible, but conjecturally moral, and certainly depressing. Once set agoing, she ran down like an alarm-clock. We awaited her subsidence as that of a shower or other inevitable natural phenomenon. More refreshing was the talk of a tall returned Californian, who told us, among other things, that "he should n't mind Panahmy's bein' sunk, ollers providin' there warn't none of *our* folks onto it when it went down!"

Our landlady's exhibition of her daughter puts me in mind of something similar, yet oddly different, which happened to Storg and me at Palestrina. We happened to praise the beauty of our stout *locandiera's* little girl. "Ah, she is nothing to her elder sister just married," said the mother. "If you could see *her!* She is bella, *bella*, BELLA!" We thought no more of it; but after dinner, the good creature, with no warning but a tap at the door and a humble *con permesso*, brought her in all her bravery, and showed her off to us as simply and naturally as if she had been a picture. The girl, who was both beautiful and modest, bore it with the dignified *aplomb* of a statue. She knew we admired her, and liked it, but with the indifference of a rose. There is something very charming, I think, in this wholly unsophisticated consciousness, with no alloy of vanity or coquetry.

A FEW BITS OF ROMAN MOSAIC.

BYRON hit the white, which he often shot very wide of in his Italian Guide-Book, when he called Rome " my country." But it is a feeling which comes to one slowly, and is absorbed into one's system during a long residence. Perhaps one does not feel it till he has gone away, as things always seem fairer when we look back at them, and it is out of that inaccessible tower of the past that Longing leans and beckons. However it be, Fancy gets a rude shock at entering Rome, which it takes her a great while to get over. She has gradually made herself believe that she is approaching a city of the dead, and has seen nothing on the road from Civita Vecchia to disturb that theory. Milestones, with "Via Aurelia" carved upon them, have confirmed it. It is eighteen hundred years ago with her, and on the dial of time the shadow has not yet trembled over the line that marks the beginning of the first century. She arrives at the gate, and a dirty, blue man, with a cocked hat and a white sword-belt, asks for her passport. Then another man, as like the first as one spoon is like its fellow, and having, like him, the look of being run in a mould, tells her that she must go to the custom-house. It is as if a ghost, who had scarcely recovered from the jar of hearing Charon say, " I 'll trouble you for your obolus, if you please," should have his portmanteau seized by the Stygian tide-waiters to be searched. Is there anything, then, contraband of death ? asks poor Fancy of herself.

But it is the misfortune (or the safeguard) of the English mind that Fancy is always an outlaw, liable to be laid by the heels wherever Constable Common Sense can catch her. She submits quietly as the postilion cries, "*Yee-ip!*" and cracks his whip, and the rattle over the pavement begins, struggles a moment when the pillars of the colonnade stalk ghostly by in the moonlight, and finally gives up all for lost when she sees Bernini's angels polking on their pedestals along the sides of the Ponte Sant' Angelo with the emblems of the Passion in their arms.

You are in Rome, of course; the *sbirro* said so, the *doganiere* bowed it, and the postilion swore it; but it is a Rome of modern houses, muddy streets, dingy *caffès*, cigar-smokers, and French soldiers, the manifest junior of Florence. And yet full of anachronisms, for in a little while you pass the column of Antoninus, find the *Dogana* in an ancient temple whose furrowed pillars show through the recent plaster, and feel as if you saw the statue of Minerva in a Paris bonnet. You are driven to a hotel where all the barbarian languages are spoken in one wild conglomerate by the *Commissionnaire*, have your dinner wholly in French, and wake the next morning dreaming of the Tenth Legion, to see a regiment of *Chasseurs de Vincennes* trotting by.

For a few days one undergoes a tremendous recoil. Other places have a distinct meaning. London is the visible throne of King Stock; Versailles is the apotheosis of one of Louis XIV.'s cast periwigs; Florence and Pisa are cities of the Middle Ages; but Rome seems to be a parody upon itself. The ticket that admits you to see the starting of the horses at carnival, has S. P. Q. R. at the top of it, and you give the *custode* a paul for showing you the wolf that suckled Romulus and Remus. The *Senatus* seems to be a score or so of elderly gentlemen in scarlet, and the *Populusque Romanus* a swarm of nasty friars.

But there is something more than mere earth in the spot where great deeds have been done. The surveyor cannot give the true dimensions of Marathon or Lexington, for they are not reducible to square acres. Dead glory and greatness leave ghosts behind them, and departed empire has a metempsychosis, if nothing else has. Its spirit haunts the grave, and waits, and waits till at last it finds a body to its mind, slips into it, and historians moralize on the fluctuation of human affairs. By and by, perhaps, enough observations will have been recorded to assure us that these recurrences are firmamental, and historionomers will have measured accurately the sidereal years of races. When that is once done, events will move with the quiet of an orrery, and nations will consent to their peridynamis and apodynamis with planetary composure.

Be this as it may, you become gradually aware of the presence of this imperial ghost among the Roman ruins. You receive hints and startles of it through the senses first, as the horse always shies at the apparition before the rider can see it. Then, little by little, you become assured of it, and seem to hear the brush of its mantle through some hall of Caracalla's baths, or one of those other solitudes of Rome. And those solitudes are with out a parallel; for it is not the mere absence of man, but the sense of his departure, that makes a profound loneliness. Musing upon them, you cannot but feel the shadow of that disembodied empire, and, remembering how the foundations of the Capitol were laid where a head was turned up, you are impelled to prophesy that the Idea of Rome will incarnate itself again as soon as an Italian brain is found large enough to hold it, and to give unity to those discordant members.

But, though I intend to observe no regular pattern in my Roman mosaic, which will resemble more what one finds in his pockets after a walk, — a pagan cube or two from the palaces of the Cæsars, a few Byzantine bits, given with many shrugs of secrecy by a lay-brother at San Paolo *fuori le mura*, and a few more (quite as ancient) from the manufactory at the Vatican, — it seems natural to begin what one has to say of Rome with something about St. Peter's; for the saint sits at the gate here as well as in Paradise.

It is very common for people to say that they are disappointed in the first sight of St. Peter's; and one hears much the same about Niagara. I cannot help thinking that the fault is in themselves; and that if the church and the cataract were in the habit of giving away their thoughts with that rash generosity which characterizes tourists, they might perhaps say of their visitors, "Well, if *you* are those men of whom we have heard so much, we are a little disappointed, to tell the truth!" The refined tourist expects somewhat too much when he takes it for granted that St. Peter's will at once decorate him with the order of imagination, just as Victoria knights an alderman when he presents an address. Or perhaps he has been getting up a little architecture on the road from Florence, and is discomfited because he does not know whether he *ought* to be pleased or not, which is very much as if he should wait to be told whether it was fresh water or salt which makes the exhaustless grace of Niagara's emerald curve, before he benignly consented to approve. It would be wiser, perhaps, for him to consider whether, if Michael Angelo had had the building of *him*, his own personal style would not have been more impressive.

It is not to be doubted that minds are of as many different orders as cathedrals, and that the Gothic imagination is vexed and discommoded in the vain endeavor to flatten its pinnacles, and fit itself into the round Roman arches. But if it be impossible for a man to like everything, it is quite possible for him to avoid being driven mad by what does not please him; nay, it is the imperative duty of a wise man to find out what that secret is which makes a thing pleasing to another. In approaching St. Peter's, one must take his Protestant shoes off his feet, and leave them behind him, in the Piazza Rusticucci. Otherwise the great Basilica, with those outstretching colonnades of Bramante, will seem to be a bloated spider lying in wait for him, the poor Reformed fly. As he lifts the heavy leathern flapper over the door, and is discharged into the interior by its impetuous recoil, let him disburden his mind altogether of stone and mortar, and think only that he is standing before the throne of a dynasty which, even in its decay, is the most powerful the world ever saw. Mason-work is all very well in itself, but it has nothing to do with the affair at present in hand.

Suppose that a man in pouring down a glass of claret could drink the South of France, that he could so disintegrate the wine by the force of imagination as to taste in it all the clustered beauty and bloom of the grape, all the dance and song and sunburnt jollity of the vintage. Or suppose that in eating bread he could transubstantiate it with the tender blade of spring, the gleam-flitted corn-ocean of summer, the royal autumn, with its golden beard, and the merry funerals of harvest. This is what the great poets do for us, we cannot tell now, with their fatally-chosen words, crowding the happy veins of language again with all the life and meaning and music that had been dribbling away from them since Adam. And this is what the Roman Church does for religion, feeding the soul not with the essential religious sentiment, not with a drop or two of the tincture of worship, but making us feel one by one all those original elements of which worship is composed; not bringing the end to us, but making us pass over and feel beneath our feet all the golden rounds of the ladder by which the climbing generations have reached that end; not handing us drily a dead and extinguished Q. E. D., but letting it rather declare itself by the glory with which it interfuses the incense-clouds of wonder and aspiration and beauty in which it is veiled. The secret of her power is typified in the mystery of the Real Presence. She is the only church that has been loyal to the heart and soul of man, that has clung to her faith in the imagination, and that would not give over her symbols and images and sacred vessels to the perilous keeping of the iconoclast

Understanding. She has never lost sight of the truth, that the product human nature is composed of the sum of flesh and spirit, and has accordingly regarded both this world and the next as the constituents of that other world which we possess by faith. She knows that poor Panza, the body, has his kitchen longings and visions, as well as Quixote, the soul, his ethereal, and has wit enough to supply him with the visible, tangible raw material of imagination. She is the only poet among the churches, and, while Protestantism is unrolling a pocket surveyor's-plan, takes her votary to the pinnacle of her temple, and shows him meadow, upland, and tillage, cloudy heaps of forest clasped with the river's jewelled arm, hillsides white with the perpetual snow of flocks, and, beyond all, the interminable heave of the unknown ocean. Her empire may be traced upon the map by the boundaries of races; the understanding is her great foe; and it is the people whose vocabulary was incomplete till they had invented the arch·

word Humbug that defies her. With that leaden bullet John Bull can bring down Sentiment when she flies her highest. And the more the pity for John Bull. One of these days some one whose eyes are sharp enough will read in the Times a standing advertisement, — "Lost, strayed, or stolen from the farm-yard of the subscriber the valuable horse Pegasus. Probably has on him part of a new plough-harness, as that is also missing. A suitable reward, etc.   J. Bull."

Protestantism reverses the poetical process I have spoken of above, and gives not even the bread of life, but instead of it the alcohol, or distilled intellectual result. This was very well so long as Protestantism continued to protest; for enthusiasm sublimates the understanding into imagination. But now that she also has become an establishment, she begins to perceive that she made a blunder in trusting herself to the intellect alone. She is beginning to feel her way back again, as one notices in Puseyism, and other such hints

One is put upon reflection when he sees burly Englishmen, who dine on beef and porter every day, marching proudly through Saint Peter's on Palm Sunday, with those frightfully artificial palm-branches in their hands. Romanism wisely provides for the childish in men.

Therefore I say again, that one must lay aside his Protestantism in order to have a true feeling of Saint Peter's. Here in Rome is the laboratory of that mysterious enchantress, who has known so well how to adapt herself to all the wants, or, if you will, the weaknesses of human nature, making the retirement of the convent-cell a merit to the solitary, the scourge or the fast a piety to the ascetic, the enjoyment of pomp and music and incense a religious act in the sensual, and furnishing for the very soul itself a *confidante* in that ear of the dumb confessional, where it may securely disburden itself of its sins and sorrows. And the dome of St. Peter's is the magic circle within which she works her most potent in cantations. I confess that I could not enter it alone without a kind of awe.

But, setting entirely aside the effect of this church upon the imagination, it is wonderful, if one consider it only materially. Michael Angelo created a new world in which everything was colossal, and it might seem that he built this as a fit temple for those gigantic figures with which he peopled it to worship in. Here his Moses should be high-priest, the service should be chanted by his prophets and sibyls, and those great pagans should be brought hither from San Lorenzo in Florence, to receive baptism.

However unsatisfactory in other matters, statistics are of service here. I have seen a refined tourist who entered, Murray in hand, sternly resolved to have St. Peter's look small, brought to terms at once by being told that the canopy over the high altar (looking very like a four-post bedstead) was ninety-eight feet high. If he still obstinates himself, he is finished by being made to measure one of the marble *putti*, which look like rather stoutish babies, and are found to be six feet, every sculptor's son of them. This ceremony is the more interesting, as it enables him to satisfy the guide of his proficiency in the Italian tongue by calling them *putty* at every convenient opportunity. Otherwise both he and his assistant terrify each other into mutual unintelligibility with that *lingua franca* of the English-speaking traveller, which is supposed to bear some remote affinity to the French language, of which both parties are as ignorant as an American Ambassador.

Murray gives all these little statistical nudges to the Anglo-Saxon imagination; but he knows that its finest nerves are in the pocket, and accordingly ends by telling you how much the church cost. I forget how much it is; but it cannot be more, I fancy, than the English national debt multiplied into itself three hundred and sixty-five times. If the pilgrim, honestly anxious for a sensation, will work out this little sum, he will be sure to receive all that enlargement of the imaginative faculty which arithmetic can give him. Perhaps the most dilating fact, after all, is that this architectural world has also a separate atmosphere, distinct from that of Rome by some ten degrees, and unvarying through the year.

I think that, on the whole, Jonathan gets ready to be pleased with St. Peter's sooner than Bull. Accustomed to our lath and plaster expedients for churches, the portable sentry-boxes of Zion, mere solidity and permanence are pleasurable in themselves; and if he get grandeur also, he has Gospel measure. Besides, it is easy for Jonathan to travel. He is one drop of a fluid mass, who knows where his home is to-day, but can make no guess of where it may be to-morrow. Even in a form of government he only takes lodgings for the night, and is ready to pay his bill and be off in the morning. He should take his motto from Bishop Golias's "*Mihi est propositum in tabernâ mori*," though not in the sufistic sense of that misunderstood Churchman. But Bul.

can seldom be said to travel at all, since the first step of a true traveller is out of himself. He plays cricket and hunts foxes on the Campagna, makes entries in his betting-book while the Pope is giving his benediction, and points out Lord Calico to you awfully during the Sistine *Miserere*. If he let his beard grow, it always has a startled air, as if it suddenly remembered its treason to Sheffield, and only makes him look more English than ever. A masquerade is impossible to him, and his fancy balls are the solemnest facts in the world. Accordingly, he enters St. Peter's with the dome of St. Paul's drawn tight over his eyes, like a criminal's cap, and ready for instant execution rather than confess that the English Wren had not a stronger wing than the Italian Angel. I like this in Bull, and it renders him the pleasantest of travelling-companions; for he makes you take England along with you, and thus you have two countries at once. And one must not forget in an Italian inn that it is to Bull he owes the clean napkins and sheets, and the privilege of his morning bath. Nor should Bull himself fail to remember that he ate with his fingers till the Italian gave him a fork.

Browning has given the best picture of St. Peter's on a festival-day, sketching it with a few verses in his large style. And doubtless it is the scene of the grandest spectacles which the world can see in these latter days. Those Easter pomps, where the antique world marches visibly before you in gilded mail and crimson doublet, refresh the eyes, and are good so long as they continue to be merely spectacle. But if one think for a moment of the servant of the servants of the Lord in cloth of gold, borne on men's shoulders, or of the children receiving the blessing of their Holy Father, with a regiment of French soldiers to protect the father from the children, it becomes a little sad. If one would feel the full meaning of those ceremonials, however, let him consider the coincidences between the Romish and the Buddhist forms of worship, and remembering that the Pope is the direct heir, through the Pontifex Maximus, of rites that were ancient when the Etruscans were modern, he will look with a feeling deeper than curiosity upon forms which record the earliest conquests of the Invisible, the first triumphs of mind over muscle.

To me the noon silence and solitude of St. Peter's were most impressive, when the sunlight, made visible by the mist of the ever-burning lamps in which it was entangled, hovered under the dome like the holy dove goldenly descending. Very grand also is the twilight, when all outlines melt into mysterious vastness, and the arches expand and lose themselves in the deepening shadow. Then, standing in the desert transept, you hear the far-off vespers swell and die like low breathings of the sea on some conjectured shore.

As the sky is supposed to scatter its golden star-pollen once every year in meteoric showers, so the dome of St. Peter's has its annual efflorescence of fire. This illumination is the great show of Papal Rome. Just after sunset,

I stood upon the Trinità dei Monti and saw the little drops of pale light creeping downward from the cross and trickling over the dome. Then, as the sky darkened behind, it seemed as if the setting sun had lodged upon the horizon and there burned out, the fire still clinging to his massy ribs. And when the change from the silver to the golden illumination came, it was as if the breeze had fanned the embers into flame again.

Bitten with the Anglo-Saxon gadfly that drives us all to disenchant artifice, and see the springs that fix it on, I walked down to get a nearer look. My next glimpse was from the bridge of Sant' Angelo; but there was no time nor space for pause. Foot-passengers crowding hither and thither, as they heard the shout of *Avanti!* from the mile of coachmen behind, dragoon-horses curtsying backward just where there were most women and children to be flattened, and the dome drawing all eyes and thoughts the wrong way, made a hubbub to be got out of at any desperate hazard. Besides, one could not help feeling nervously hurried; for it seemed quite plain to everybody that this starry apparition must be as momentary as it was wonderful, and that we should find it vanished when we reached the piazza. But suddenly you stand in front of it, and see the soft travertine of the front suffused with a tremulous, glooming glow, a mildened glory, as if the building breathed, and so transmuted its shadow into soft pulses of light.

After wondering long enough, I went back to the Pincio, and watched it for an hour longer. But I did not wish to see it go out. It seemed better to go home and leave it still trembling, so that I could fancy a kind of permanence in it, and half believe I should find it there again some lucky evening. Before leaving it altogether, I went away to cool my eyes with darkness, and came back several times; and every time it was a new miracle, the more so that it was a human piece of faëry-work. Beautiful as fire is in itself, I suspect that part of the pleasure is metaphysical, and that the sense of playing with an element which can be so terrible adds to the zest of the spectacle. And then fire is not the least degraded by it, because it is not utilized. If beauty were in use, the factory would add a grace to the river, and we should turn from the fire-writing on the wall of heaven to look at a message printed by the magnetic telegraph. There may be a beauty in the use itself; but utilization is always downward, and it is this feeling that makes Schiller's Pegasus in yoke so universally pleasing. So long as the curse of work clings to man, he will see beauty only in play. The capital of the most frugal commonwealth in the world burns up five thousand dollars a year in gunpowder, and nobody murmurs. Provident Judas wished to utilize the ointment, but the Teacher would rather that it should be wasted in poem.

The best lesson in æsthetics I ever got (and, like most good lessons, it fell from the lips of no regular professor) was from an Irishman on the day the Nymph Cochituate was formally introduced to the people of Boston. I made one with other rustics in the streets, admiring the dignitaries in coaches with as much Christian charity as is consistent with an elbow in the pit of your stomach and a heel on that toe which is your only inheritance from two excellent grandfathers. Among other allegorical phenomena, there came along what I should have called a hay-cart, if I had not known it was a triumphal car, filled with that fairest variety of mortal grass which with us is apt to spindle so soon into a somewhat sapless womanhood. Thirty-odd young maidens in white gowns, with blue sashes and pink wreaths of French crape, represented the United States. (How shall we limit our number, by the way, if ever Utah be admitted?) The ship, the printing-press, even the wondrous train of express-wagons, and other solid bits of civic fantasy, had left my Hibernian neighbor unmoved. But this brought him down. Turning to me, as the most appreciative public for the moment, with face of as much delight as if his head had been broken, he cried, "Now this is *raly* beautiful! Tothally regyardless uv expinse!" Methought my shirt-sleeved lecturer on the Beautiful had hit at least one nail full on the head. Voltaire but epigrammatized the same thought when he said, *Le superflu, chose très-necessaire.*

As for the ceremonies of the Church, one need not waste time in seeing many of them. There is a dreary sameness in them, and one can take an hour here and an hour there, as it pleases him, just as sure of finding the same pattern as he would be in the first or last yard of a roll of printed cotton. For myself, I do not like to go and look with mere curiosity at what is sacred and solemn to others. To how many these Roman shows are sacred, I cannot guess; but certainly the Romans do not value them much. I walked out to the grotto of Egeria on Easter Sunday, that I might not be tempted down to St. Peter's to see the mock ery of Pio Nono's benediction. It is certainly Christian, for he blesses them that curse him, and does all the good which the waving of his fingers can do to people who would use him despitefully if they had the chance. I told an Italian servant she might have the day; but she said she did not care for it.

"But," urged I, "will you not go to receive the blessing of the Holy Father?"

"No, sir."

"Do you not wish it?"

"Not in the least: *his* blessing would do me no good. If I get the blessing of Heaven, it will serve my turn."

There were three families of foreigners in our house, and I believe none of the Italian servants went to St. Peter's that day. Yet they commonly speak kindly of Pius. I have heard the same phrase from several Italians of the working-class. "He is a good man," they said, "but ill-led."

What one sees in the streets of Rome is worth more than what one sees in the churches.

The churches themselves are generally ugly. St. Peter's has crushed all the life out of architectural genius, and all the modern churches look as if they were swelling themselves in imitation of the great Basilica. There is a clumsy magnificence about them, and their heaviness oppresses you. Their marble incrustations look like a kind of architectural elephantiasis, and the parts are puffy with a dropsical want of proportion. There is none of the spring and soar which one may see even in the Lombard churches, and a Roman column standing near one of them, slim and gentlemanlike, satirizes silently their tawdry *parvenu*ism. Attempts at mere bigness are ridiculous in a city where the Colosseum still yawns in craterlike ruin, and where Michael Angelo made a noble church out of a single room in Diocletian's baths.

Shall I confess it? Michael Angelo seems to me, in his angry reaction against sentimental beauty, to have mistaken bulk and brawn for the antithesis of feebleness. He is the apostle of the exaggerated, the Victor Hugo of painting and sculpture. I have a feeling that rivalry was a more powerful motive with him than love of art, that he had the conscious intention to be original, which seldom leads to anything better than being extravagant. The show of muscle proves strength, not power; and force for mere force's sake in art makes one think of Milo caught in his own log. This is my second thought, and strikes me as perhaps somewhat niggardly toward one in whom you cannot help feeling there was so vast a possibility. And then his Eve, his David, his Sibyls, his Prophets, his Sonnets. Well, I take it all back, and come round to St. Peter's again just to hint that I doubt about domes. In Rome they are so much the fashion that I felt as if they were the *goître* of architecture. Generally they look heavy. Those on St. Mark's in Venice are the only light ones I ever saw, and they look almost airy, like tents puffed out with wind. I suppose one must be satisfied with the interior effect, which is certainly noble in St. Peter's. But for impressiveness both within and without there is nothing like a Gothic cathedral for me, nothing that crowns a city so nobly, or makes such an island of twilight silence in the midst of its noonday clamors.

Now as to what one sees in the streets, the beggars are certainly the first things that draw the eye. Beggary is an institution here. The Church has sanctified it by the establishment of mendicant orders, and indeed it is the natural result of a social system where the non-producing class makes not only the laws, but the ideas. The beggars of Rome go far toward proving the diversity of origin in mankind, for on them surely the curse of Adam never fell. It is easier to fancy that Adam *Vaurien*, the first tenant of the Fool's Paradise, after sucking his thumbs for a thousand years, took to wife Eve *Faniente*, and became the progenitor of this race, to whom also he left a calendar in which three hundred and sixty-five days in the year were made feasts, sacred from all secular labor. Accordingly, they not merely do nothing, but they do it assiduously and almost with religious fervor. I have seen ancient members of this sect as constant at their accustomed street-corner as the bit of broken column on which they sat; and when a man does this in rainy weather, as rainy weather is in Rome, he has the spirit of a fanatic and martyr.

It is not that the Italians are a lazy people. On the contrary, I am satisfied that they are industrious so far as they are allowed to be. But, as I said before, when a Roman does nothing, he does it in the high Roman fashion. A friend of mine was having one of his rooms arranged for a private theatre, and sent for a person who was said to be an expert in the business to do it for him. After a day's trial, he was satisfied that his lieutenant was rather a hinderance than a help, and resolved to dismiss him.

"What is your charge for your day's services?"

"Two scudi, sir."

"Two scudi! Five pauls would be too much. You have done nothing but stand with your hands in your pockets and get in the way of other people."

"Lordship is perfectly right; but *that* is my way of working."

It is impossible for a stranger to say who may *not* beg in Rome. It seems to be a sudden madness that may seize any one at the sight of a foreigner. You see a very respectable-looking person in the street, and it is odds but, as you pass him, his hat comes off, his whole figure suddenly dilapidates itself, assuming a tremble of professional weakness, and you hear the everlasting *qualche cosa per carità!* You are in doubt whether to drop a bajoccho into the next cardinal's hat which offers you its sacred cavity in answer to your salute. You begin to believe that the hat was invented for the sole purpose of ingulfing coppers, and that its highest type is the grea* *Triregno* itself, into which the pence of Peter rattle.

But you soon learn to distinguish the established beggars, and to the three professions elsewhere considered liberal you add a fourth for this latitude, — mendicancy. Its professors look upon themselves as a kind of guild which ought to be protected by the government. I fell into talk with a woman who begged of me in the Colosseum. Among other things she complained that the government did not at all consider the poor.

"Where is the government that does?" I said.

"*Eh già!* Excellency; but this government lets beggars from the country come into Rome, which is a great injury to the trade of us born Romans. There is Beppo, for example; he is a man of property in his own town, and has a dinner of three courses every day. He has portioned two daughters with three thousand scudi each, and left Rome during the time of the Republic with the rest of the nobility."

At first, one is shocked and pained at the exhibition of deformities in the street But by and by he comes to look upon them with little more emotion than is excited by seeing the tools of any other trade. The melancholy of the beggars is purely a matter of business; and they look upon their maims as Fortunatus purses, which will always give them money. A withered arm they present to you as a highwayman would his pistol; a *goitre* is a life-annuity; a St. Vitus dance is as good as an engagement as *prima ballerina* at the Apollo; and to have no legs at all is to stand on the best footing with fortune. They are a merry race, on the whole, and quick-witted, like the rest of their countrymen. I believe the regular fee for a beggar is a *quattrino*, about a quarter of a cent; but they expect more of foreigners. A friend of mine once gave one of these tiny coins to an old woman; she delicately expressed her resentment by exclaiming, "Thanks, *signoria*. God will reward *even* you!"

A begging friar came to me one day with a subscription for repairing his convent. "Ah, but I am a heretic," said I. "Undoubtedly," with a shrug, implying a respectful acknowledgment of a foreigner's right to choose warm and dry lodgings in the other world as well as in this, "but your money is perfectly orthodox."

Another favorite way of doing nothing is to excavate the Forum. I think the *Fanientes* like this all the better, because it seems a kind of satire upon work, as the witches parody the Christian offices of devotion at their Sabbath. A score or so of old men in voluminous cloaks shift the earth from one side of a large pit to the other, in a manner so leisurely that it is positive repose to look at them. The most bigoted anti-Fourierist might acknowledge this to be attractive industry.

One conscript father trails a small barrow up to another, who stands leaning on a long spade. Arriving, he fumbles for his snuffbox, and offers it deliberately to his friend. Each takes an ample pinch, and both seat themselves to await the result. If one should sneeze, he receives the *Felicità!* of the other⋅ and, after allowing the titillation to subside, he replies, *Grazia!* Then follows a little conversation, and then they prepare to load. But it occurs to the barrow-driver that this is a good opportunity to fill and light his pipe; and to do so conveniently he needs his barrow to sit upon. He draws a few whiffs, and a little more conversation takes place. The barrow is now ready; but first the wielder of the spade will fill *his* pipe also. This done, more whiffs and more conversation. Then a spoonful of earth is thrown into the barrow, and it starts on its return. But midway it meets an empty barrow, and both stop to go through the snuff-box ceremonial once more, and to discuss whatever new thing has occurred in the excavation since their last encounter. And so it goes on all day.

As I see more of material antiquity, I begin to suspect that my interest in it is mostly factitious. The relations of races to the physical world (only to be studied fruitfully on the spot) do not excite in me an interest at all proportionate to that I feel in their influence on the moral advance of mankind, which one may as easily trace in his own library as on the spot. The only useful remark I remember to have made here is, that, the situation of Rome being far less strong than that of any city of the Etruscan league, it must have been built where it is for purposes of commerce. It is the most defensible point near the mouth of the Tiber. It is only as rival trades-folk that Rome and Carthage had any comprehensible cause of quarrel. It is only as a commercial people that we can understand the early tendency of the Romans towards democracy. As for antiquity, after reading history, one is haunted by a discomforting suspicion that the names so painfully deciphered in hieroglyphic or arrow-head inscriptions are only so many more Smiths and Browns masking it in unknown tongues. Moreover, if we Yankees are twitted with not knowing the difference between *big* and *great*, may not those of us who have learned it turn round on many a monument over here with the same reproach? I confess I am beginning to sympathize with a countryman of ours from Michigan, who asked our Minister to direct him to a specimen ruin and a specimen gallery, that he might see and be rid of them once for all. I saw three young Englishmen going through the Vatican by catalogue and number, the other day, in a fashion which John Bull is apt to consider exclusively American. "Number 300!" says the one with catalogue and pencil, "have you seen it?" "Yes," answer his two comrades, and, checking it off, he goes on with Number 301. Having witnessed the unavailing agonies of many Anglo-Saxons from both sides of the Atlantic in their effort to have the correct sensation before many hideous examples of antique bad taste, my heart warmed toward my business-like British cousins, who were doing their æsthetics in this thrifty auctioneer fashion. Our cart-before-horse education, which makes us more familiar with the history and literature of Greeks and Romans than with those of our own ancestry, (though there is nothing in ancient art to match Shakespeare or a Gothic minster,) makes us the gulls of what we call classical antiquity. In sculpture, to be sure, they have us on the hip. Europe were worth visiting, if only to be rid of this one old man of the sea.

I am not ashamed to confess a singular sympathy with what are known as the Middle Ages. I cannot help thinking that few periods have left behind them such traces of inventiveness and power. Nothing is more tiresome than the sameness of modern cities; and it has often struck me that this must also have been true of those ancient ones in which Greek architecture or its derivatives prevailed,— true at least as respects public buildings. But mediæval towns, especially in Italy, even when only fifty miles asunder, have an individuality of character as marked as that of trees. Nor is it merely this originality that attracts me, but likewise the sense that, however old, they are nearer to me in being modern and Christian. I find it harder to bridge over the gulf of Paganism than of centuries. Apart from any difference in the men, I had a far deeper emotion when I stood on the *Sasso di Dante*, than at Horace's Sabine farm or by the tomb of Virgil. The latter, indeed, interested me chiefly by its association with comparatively modern legend; and one of the buildings I am most glad to have seen in Rome is the Bear Inn, where Montaigne lodged on his arrival.

I think it must have been for some such reason that I liked my Florentine better than my Roman walks, though I am vastly more contented with merely being in Rome. Florence is more noisy; indeed, I think it the noisiest town I was ever in. What with the continual jangling of its bells, the rattle of Austrian drums, and the street-cries, *Ancora mi raccapriccia*. The Italians are a vocifer ous people, and most so among them the Florentines. Walking through a back street one day, I saw an old woman higgling with a peripatetic dealer, who, at every interval afforded him by the remarks of his veteran antagonist, would tip his head on one side, and shout, with a kind of wondering enthusiasm, as if he could hardly trust the evidence of his own senses to such loveliness, *O, che bellezza! che belle-e-ezza!* The two had been contending as obstinately as the Greeks and Trojans over the body of Patroclus, and I was curious to know what was the object of so much desire on the one side and admiration on the other. It was a half-dozen of weazeny baked pears, beggarly remnant of the day's traffic. Another time I stopped before a stall, debating whether to buy some fine-looking peaches. Before I had made up my mind, the vender, a stout fellow, with a voice like a prize-bull of Bashan, opened a mouth round and large as the muzzle of a blunderbuss, and let fly into my ear the following pertinent observation: "*Belle pesche! belle pe-e-esche!*" (*crescendo.*) I stared at him in stunned bewilderment; but, seeing that he had reloaded and was about to fire again, took to my heels, the exploded syllables rattling after me like so many buckshot. A single turnip is argument enough with them till midnight; nay, I have heard a ruffian yelling over a covered basket, which, I am convinced, was empty, and only carried as an excuse for his stupendous vocalism. It never struck me before what a quiet people Americans are.

Of the pleasant places within easy walk of Rome, I prefer the garden of the Villa Albani, as being most Italian. One does not go to Italy for examples of Price on the Picturesque. Compared with landscape-gardening, it is Racine to Shakespeare, I grant; but it has its own charm, nevertheless. I like the balustraded terraces, the sun-proof laurel walks, the vases and statues. It is only in such a climate that it does not seem inhuman to thrust a naked statue out of doors. Not to speak of their incongruity, how dreary do those white figures look at Fountains Abbey in that shrewd Yorkshire atmosphere! To put them there shows the same bad taste that led Prince Polonia, as Thackeray calls him, to build an artificial ruin within a mile of Rome. But I doubt if the Italian garden will bear transplantation. Farther north, or under a less constant sunshine, it is but half-hardy at the best. Within the city, the garden of the French Academy is my favorite retreat, because little frequented; and there is an arbor there in which I have read comfortably (sitting where the sun could reach me) in January. By the way, there is something very agreeable in the way these people have of making a kind of fireside of the sunshine. With us it is either too hot or too cool, or we are too busy. But, on the other hand, they have no such thing as a chimney-corner.

Of course I haunt the collections of art faithfully; but my favorite gallery, after all, is the street. There I always find something entertaining, at least. The other day, on my way to the Colonna Palace, I passed the Fountain of Trevi, from which the water is now shut off on account of repairs to the aqueduct. A scanty rill of soap-sudsy water still trickled from one of the conduits, and, seeing a crowd, I stopped to find out what nothing or other had gathered it. One charm of Rome is that nobody has anything in particular to do, or, if he has, can always stop doing it on the slightest pretext. I found that some eels had been discovered, and a very vivacious hunt was going on, the chief Nimrods being boys. I happened to be the first to see a huge eel wriggling from the mouth of a pipe, and pointed him out. Two lads at once rushed upon him. One essayed the capture with his naked hands, the other, more provident, had armed himself with a rag of woollen cloth with which to maintain his grip more securely. Hardly had this latter arrested his slippery prize, when a ragged rascal, watching his opportunity, snatched away the prize, and instantly secured t by thrusting the head into his mouth, and closing on it a set of teeth like an ivory vice. But alas for ill-got gain! Rob Roy's

> "Good old plan,
> That he should take who has the power,
> And he should keep who can,"

did not serve here. There is scarce a square rood in Rome without one or more stately cocked hats in it, emblems of authority and police. I saw the flash of the snow-white cross-belts, gleaming through that dingy crowd like the *panache* of Henri Quatre at Ivry, I saw the mad plunge of the canvas-shielded head-piece, sacred and terrible as that of Gessler; and while the greedy throng were dancing about the anguilliceps, each taking his chance twitch at the undulating object of all wishes, the captor dodging his head hither and thither, (vulnerable, like Achilles, only in his 'eel, as a British tourist would say,) a pair of broad blue shoulders parted the assailants as a ship's bows part a wave, a pair of blue arms, terminating in gloves of Berlin thread, were stretched forth, not in benediction, one hand grasped the slippery Briseis by the waist, the other bestowed a cuff on the jaw-bone of Achilles, which loosened (rather by its authority than its physical force) the hitherto refractory incisors, a snuffy bandanna was produced, the prisoner was deposited in this temporary watch-house, and the cocked hat sailed majestically away with the property thus sequestered for the benefit of the state.

> "Gaudeant anguillæ si mortuus sit homo ille,
> Qui, quasi morte reas, excruciabat eas!"

If you have got through that last sentence without stopping for breath, you are fit to begin on the Homer of Chapman, who, both as translator and author, has the longest wind, (especially for a comparison,) without being long-winded, of all writers I know anything of, not excepting Jeremy Taylor.

www.ingramcontent.com/pod-product-compliance
Lightning Source LLC
Chambersburg PA
CBHW021206230426
43667CB00006B/576